JAMAICAN PEOPLE, PLACES & SYMBOLS—CARIBBEAN JEWELS

A travel guide with timeless Jamaican proverbs and sayings, folk songs, Flora and fauna

Andrea Campbell & Richmond Tyser

JAMAICAN PEOPLE, PLACES & SYMBOLS—CARIBBEAN JEWELS

A travel guide with timeless Jamaican proverbs and sayings, folk songs, flora and fauna

Andrea Campbell & Richmond Tyser

Cover image: Mammee Bay, Ocho Rios, Jamaica
Courtesy of Staicy Androose

Pocket Learner Publishing

Copyright © 2023 Andrea Campbell and Richmond Tyser

The content of this book may not be reproduced, duplicated or transmitted without direct written permission from the author or publisher. Under no circumstances will any blame or legal responsibility be held against the publisher, or author, for any damages, reparation, or monetary loss due to the information contained within this book; either directly or indirectly. You are responsible for your own choices, actions, and results.

Legal Notice:

This book is copyright protected and is only for personal use. You cannot amend, distribute, sell, use, quote or paraphrase any part, of this book without the consent of the author or publisher.

Disclaimer Notice:

Please note the information contained in this text is for educational and entertainment purposes only. All effort has been executed to present accurate, up-to-date, and reliable, complete information. No warranties of any kind are declared or implied. Readers acknowledge that the author is not engaging in the rendering of legal, financial, medical, or professional advice. The content within this book has been derived from various sources. Please consult a licensed professional before attempting any techniques outlined in this book.

By reading this document, the reader agrees that under no circumstances is the author responsible for any losses, direct or indirect, which are incurred as a result of the use of the information contained within this document, including, but not limited to - errors, omissions, or inaccuracies.

ISBN: 978-1-914997-34-1 (hc)   978-1-914997-35-8 (sc)

Acknowledgements

We would like to thank the editors – Janet Crick of Jamaica Culinary Tours (https://jamaicaculinarytours.com) and the late Horace Whittaker, JP.

We are also grateful to our families and all those who made our work possible through their contribution, love and support.

Thanks also for the contributions from Wellesley Gayle, author and publisher of https://www.my-island-jamaica.com/ and to the Jamaica Tourist Board.

Dedication

To the memory of my grandmother—Mrs. Iris Ingram Steele, who inspired me to live my life in the pursuit of excellence, with gratitude, and in the service of others.

I want to dedicate this book also to families everywhere who care for disabled children and adults, in their endeavor to provide inspiration and boost aspiration.

TABLE OF CONTENTS

Acknowledgements v
Dedication vi
Preface ix
Foreword xi
Introduction 1
Part I   **Proverbs And Sayings** 5
Part II   **Folk Songs** 99
Part III **Symbols, People, Places & Things** 111

   Jamaica – Land of Wood and Water 113
   Map of Jamaica 115
   National Symbols 116
   Jamaica's National Heroes 118
   Out of Many, One People 121
   National Anthem 122
   Code for use of the National Anthem 122
   National Song: I Pledge my Heart 123
   National Pledge 123
   Shorter Pledge for Schools 123
   National Prayer 124
   Ethnic Groups 125
   Governors-General of Jamaica 128
   Jamaica's Prime Ministers 129
   Distinguished Pioneers 130
   Outstanding and Distinguished Jamaicans 132
      THE ARTS 132
        – *Fine Arts* *132*
        – *Literature* *133*
        – *Music* *135*
        – *Performing Arts* *140*
        – *Visual Arts* *143*
      BEAUTY AND MODELING 143
      BUSINESS 145
      LAW 149
      SCIENCE AND MEDICINE 153
      SPORTS 158

Other Outstanding Jamaicans 163
Famous people who made Jamaica home 176
Food and Drink 178
Flora and Fauna 181
Medicinal herbs grown in Jamaica 186
Jamaica's Parishes 187
Travel Overview 195

GLOSSARY 199
INDEX 205
REFERENCES 207

Preface

If you are visiting Jamaica there is so much to do and see in this island paradise that good planning is essential. You might know about the beautiful waterfalls and beaches, the music and entertainment and perhaps the delicious and exciting food and beverages on offer. However, there is so much more to enjoy.

During your visit you might want to try a few of the following activities:

- Rum tasting
- Sailing on a bamboo raft
- Playing on picturesque golf courses
- Exploring life above ground
- Hiking in the mountains & valleys
- Plantation tours & great houses
- Equestrian activities
- Visit caves
- Adventure tours
- Bird watching
- Cultural explorations
- Music festivals
- Cycling contests
- Fashion fiestas
- Literary festivals
- Bridal shows
- Wellness festivals
- Party events

While enjoying these great activities, please bear in mind the following:

1. Jamaicans drive on the left side of the road. The speed limit is 50 km p/h (30 mph) in built-up areas, and 80 km p/h (50 mph) on highways. All drivers are required to carry a valid license. Jamaica recognizes valid International Driver's Licenses. The driver and front passenger are required to wear safety belts, and children under 3 years old must travel in infant carriers. Service stations are readily available.

2. With the many images of Rastafarians puffing away on their "ganja spliffs" and the hype surrounding medical marijuana, one might be convinced that certain practices are allowed

without repercussions. Be warned however that the use, sale and possession of narcotics are illegal.

3. Disability access is a work in progress. While some of the all-inclusive resorts are accessible you may wish to consult websites and blogs that focus on accessible travel for practical information.

4. Avoid flashing your cash and wearing expensive jewellery on road trips and excursions.

Foreword

From the first European sightings of this island paradise five and a quarter centuries ago to present day, millions of visitors have been captivated by the alluring beauty of Jamaica. First time and repeat holiday makers have confessed to being spellbound by the diversity of Jamaica's sparkling white sand beaches, majestic mountains, picturesque plains, beautiful underwater caves, rolling hills, cascading waterfalls and lush green forests. And still yet a significant number of visitors have admitted that they have been profoundly affected and even influenced by their interactions with the people and the exposure to the rich diverse culture, local cuisine, tropical fruits, fragrant rum and other delightful drinks, music and the almost never-ending entertainment and vibrant nightlife that pervades across the island.

Several world leaders and notable political thinkers who have visited the shores of Jamaica have acknowledged that they were inspired by the spirit and determination of the people. The renowned liberator of Latin America, Simon Bolivar, wrote the famous "Letter from Jamaica" in which he expressed his ideas for republican government and Latin American unity.

The celebrated Dr. Martin Luther King Jr. fell in love with Jamaica on his first trip in 1965 and declared the country the most beautiful in the world. In 1967, Dr King returned to Jamaica where he completed the manuscript of his book 'Where Do We Go from Here'. He was so moved by the multiracial, non-hierarchical nation of many different groups that he noted: One day, here in America, I hope that we will see this and we will become one big family of Americans.

Equally Nelson Mandela, the distinguished South African leader and antiapartheid revolutionary had an endearing kinship to the first country in the Western hemisphere to bring sanctions against South Africa and whose music was synonymous with the struggle against apartheid. Mandela declared on his visit to Jamaica in 1991 that it was the happiest day of his life.

There is also the other side of Jamaica that is recognized globally due to the outstanding successes of its sons and daughters of the soil and those of Jamaican heritage. We have produced world icons at almost every level including but not limited to the arts, sports, music, science, medicine, law, international relations and modelling. A section of the book highlights the outstanding achievements of Jamaicans in these areas.

Jamaican Proverbs, People and Places introduces a core part of Jamaica's cultural tradition. And whilst many may argue that that the tradition is slowly being eroded from the exposure to foreign television, merchandise and music, there is hardly any Jamaican with deep roots who will not agree that for generations their fore-parents have inundated them with proverbs to describe situations or challenges that they have faced. In true Jamaican fashion many of these sayings are enveloped in humour, yet the message is infused with lessons for upward social mobility, discipline, knowledge and wisdom. Unfortunately the advent of modern day communication devices has diminished the use of oral traditions as a means of imparting moral and educational instructions.

The purpose of this book therefore is to recapture the essence of Jamaica and reinvigorate the characteristics of pride of self, discipline, fortitude, ambition and motivation. These qualities are locked in the vast number of idioms and adages of which Jamaicans and West Indians in general can identify with. The cultural heritage of Jamaica is replete with proverbs. They epitomize a journey and a history of a people fraught with difficulties and hardship but having the tenacity, resourcefulness and willpower to overcome, knowing that 'de race ah noh fe de

Foreword

swift nor de battle fe de strong, but fe him who perseveres to de en'.

In recent times this island paradise has had its share of negative publicity as a result of a few young miscreants who have decided to put their greed and misguided self-interest above love and loyalty to country. This book has sought to bring back into focus some of the many positive contributions of its greatest assets - the people.

We must not forget the many thousands of ordinary Jamaicans who have been making an indelible mark and who have shown to the world that as Jamaicans we can achieve through vision, hard work and a determination to succeed. I hope this book will serve to inspire young Jamaicans and the Jamaican Diaspora to strive for even greater heights in the pursuit of success through honest means.

The use of proverbs to educate must not lose its value, so let us preserve our heritage while we continue to raise the Black, Green and Gold Flag, mindful that we are still at the beginning of our journey yet confident and positive in our belief that 'big tree no cut dung wid one blow'.

Jamaican Proverbs and Places should be a catalyst to generate discourse within family and communal settings and engender a sense of pride and self-awareness among Jamaicans and their descendants.

Horace W. Whittaker JP, LLM

Introduction

Jamaican Proverbs, People and Places captures over 500 adages used in Jamaica to communicate ideas about human nature, behaviour, relationships, aspirations, health, hope and survival. They convey important messages and are often used to instil discipline in children and contextualise situations for the unwitting adult - timeless, succinct, often funny phrases containing cultural symbolism that can be interpreted in various ways.

The adages represent an archive of the wit and wisdom of many generations and aim to trigger reflection and thought. In their use they are never really explained but those to whom they are directed usually understand their meaning based on the context in which they are used. They utilize imagery and draw upon a variety of flora and fauna to enrich their content. They hold valuable lessons, inspiration and wisdom that link Jamaican culture to its African past.

The ability to understand the proverbs depends on the reader's familiarity with Jamaican life. Second and third generation Jamaicans living in foreign countries may struggle to understand them in their natural state. Indeed Jamaican children at home and abroad are losing their self-awareness and sense of pride as their exposure to other cultures becomes more significant.

Although a concerted attempt has been made to render the most familiar interpretation of the proverbs, some readers will be aware of other usages and meanings based on their personal recollections and experience. In *Jamaican*

Proverb, People and Places each proverb is presented in three parts:

- **The actual proverb in its original form**
- *The literal English translation*
- The meaning it endeavours to convey.

Although every attempt is made to include only those proverbs that are uniquely Jamaican, there are several which are popular not only in Jamaica but also in other countries. Their inclusion in this collection is deliberate because they occupy a significant place in Jamaican culture. There are also some proverbs that have an established English equivalence and where known these are added for comparison and to promote clarity. There are some proverbs that can be applied in more than one context and where applicable, two meanings are presented.

Part II of the book contains a number of sayings – unique expressions used by Jamaicans to communicate, highlight and dramatise information. They demonstrate the creativity and humour of our people.

Part III will bring cheer to Jamaicans who will undoubtedly reminisce on their early days in Jamaica. Apart from singing the folk songs at school the songs were performed at many social gatherings and performances. They never fail to generate laughter and a sense of togetherness.

Part IV presents an insight into Jamaica – places, the people, their achievements, heroes, symbols, folklore, food, fauna and flora. For a tiny island nation we have had either by birth or ancestry a disproportionate number of high achievers and outstanding individuals making significant contributions both locally and globally. Many of us are

Introduction

unaware of our triumphs and successes; this section lists a few of the people who have made Jamaica proud and aims to engender a sense of pride in Jamaicans at home and abroad.

The book is also especially useful to visitors to the island with useful information about the country and what is on offer across the different parishes.

The text contains a number of images depicting Jamaican beauty spots, recent developments in the country and things Jamaican. Readers not resident on the island should enjoy the glossary which presents a small collection of Jamaican terminology and their English equivalence.

Jamaican Proverbs, People and Places aims to renew and reinvigorate Jamaican wisdom through proverbs and sayings, display the excellent contributions Jamaicans are making worldwide and showcase developments in the island for the benefit of those who have not visited in recent years. It will engender a sense of pride among all Jamaicans and evoke a feeling of nostalgia, encouraging Jamaicans, particularly those living overseas, to acknowledge and embrace their heritage and reconnect with their culture.

Part I

PROVERBS AND SAYINGS

Part I: Proverbs and Sayings

1. Ackee lub fat, ocra lub salt
Ackee loves fat, okra loves salt
People will pursue whatever they deem attractive;
Everyone has his own taste.

2. Ah fass mek anancy deh ah house tap
It's because Anancy is inquisitive why he is living in the ceiling
Mind your own business or you could find yourself in trouble or isolated.

3. Ah greedy mek fly fallaw coffin go ah hole
It's because of greed why a fly follows a coffin to the grave
Greed is the root of all evil; it can bring about your downfall.

4. Ah noh ebery chain yuh ear ah rolling calf
It's not every chain that you hear that is a rolling calf
Bad news can be exaggerated; don't always assume the worst.

5. Ah noh ebery day ah Krismus
Not every day is Christmas
You will not always get what you want.

6. Ah noh ebery rainfall mus wet yuh
It is not every rainfall that should wet you
You don't have to be a part of everything; let some things go by.

7. Ah noh ebery shut yeye ah sleep
It is not every time that you shut your eyes that you are sleeping
Appearances are not always what they seem.

8. Ah noh ebery mango gat maggige
It is not every mango that has maggots
Everyone is not the same; people have different characteristics and you shouldn't make assumptions or generalise.

9. Ah noh everyting good fi eat good fi talk
Not everything that is good to eat is also good to discuss
Some things are better left unspoken; don't repeat everything you hear!

10. Ah noh one day monkey waah wife
It's not for just one day only that a monkey wants sexual favours

It's not just once that you will want a favour; show some
gratitude to those who support you!

11. Ah noh same day leaf drap inna wahta ih rotten
It's not the same day that a leaf drops in water that it rots
Some things take time, learn to be patient;
People don't suddenly become evil, their character takes
time to develop.

12. Ah noh soh Baker buy Bowden
That is not how Baker bought Bowden
If you want a particular outcome you have to work at it;
don't expect it to happen automatically.

13. Ah noh want ah fat mek nightingale foot tan so
It's not for the lack of fat why a nightingale's feet are like that
You shouldn't judge by appearances
(Similar to: Don't judge a book by its cover).

14. Ah swif mek wass-wass noh gedder honey
It's because of haste why wasps don't gather honey
Take time to learn a job properly, then you will be able
to reap appropriate rewards.

15. All duck noh dabble inna one hole
All ducks do not dabble in the same hole
Be mindful of the fact that people belong to different social classes.

16. All kine ah fish eat man, only shaak get blame
All types of fish eat people but only sharks are blamed for it
If you have a bad reputation you will be blamed for everything,
even when you are innocent.

17. Alligetta lay egg, but im noh fowl
Alligators lay eggs but alligators are not fowls
People may engage in similar activities but that does not mean
that they are alike.

18. Alligetta shouden call hog lang mout'
An alligator should not refer to a hog as 'long mouth'
Be careful not to ridicule or belittle someone who has similar
characteristics to you.

Part I: Proverbs and Sayings

19. Ants fallaw fat, bees fallaw honey
Ants follow fat, bees follow honey
People naturally gravitate to prosperity and affluence.

20. Anyting inna dark mus com ah lite
Anything in the dark must come to light
Anything that is done in the dark will be revealed in due course.

21. Anyting tan too lang serve two master
Anything that stays too long will serve two masters
If you don't make use of what you have, someone else will.

22. Anyway ih mawga ih pap
Anywhere it becomes thin it will break
There's no point in worrying about scarce resources – make the best use of what you have.

23. A tayla nebber av a good suit
A tailor never owns a good suit
People should practise what they preach and lead by example.

24. Ax me no question ah tell yuh no lie
Ask me no question, I will tell you no lie
Avoid excessive questioning, lest you receive false information.

25. Bad fambily betta dan empty pigsty
A bad family is better than an empty pigsty
Family is important and no matter how bad you think they are, you should treasure them!

26. Bad luck woss dan obeah
Bad luck is worse than obeah
We all need some luck in life.

27. Beetle nebber right befoe hen
A beetle is never right in the sight of a hen
Your enemies will always judge you harshly.

28. Befoe dawg go widout supper, im nyam cackroach
To avoid going without supper, a dog will eat cockroaches
People will resort to unconventional measures when circumstances dictate the need.
(Similar to: Any port in a storm)

29. Begga beg from begga nebber get rich
Beggars who beg from other beggars will never get rich
Try to make friends with positive, progressive people who will inspire you to grow.

30. Behine dawg ah dawg, in front ah dawg ah Missa Dawg
Behind dog is "Dog"; in front of dog is "Mr. Dog"
People disrespect you in your absence but not generally in your presence.

31. Betta fish inna di sea dan wats already caught
There is better fish is in the sea than those that are already caught
There are always better choices available.

32. Big blanket mek man sleep late
A thick blanket causes a man to sleep late
Luxury invites complacency and a tendency to take life's blessings for granted.

33. Big massa gi ebery man im own mout fi swallow im own duckunno
Big master gave every man his own mouth to swallow his own duckunno
God blessed everyone with talents which they should endeavour to use.

34. Big tree noh cut dung wid one blow
One blow is not sufficient to cut down a big tree
Persevererance is the key; success takes time.
(Similar to: Rome wasn't built in a day)

35. Bline man see im neighba fault
A blind man sees his neighbour's faults
Too often we are blind to our own short-comings but quick to point out those of others.

36. Black fowl noh fi yuh, yuh call im jankro
If a black fowl is not yours, you will call him vulture
People tend to think that what they have is better than those of others even when it is clear that they are exactly the same.

Part I: Proverbs and Sayings

37. Blood ticka dan wahta
Blood is thicker than water
Family comes first.

38. Bowl go, buggy come
A bowl goes a buggy comes
If you give even a little you will receive a lot; be kind!

39. Bruk calabash bring new one
Break a calabash and bring a new one
Don't waste time worrying over a failed attempt, just try again.

40. Bucket wid hole ah battam noh bizniz ah rivaside
A bucket with a hole in the bottom has no business at the riverside
Keep out of people's business, especially when you have secrets yourself.

41. Bud cyaan fly pan one wing
Birds cannot fly on a single wing
People need to help each other; it is difficult to succeed all on your own.

42. Bud sing sweet fi im owna nes
Birds sing sweetly for their own nests
People save the best for themselves.

43. Bush hab aise, wall hab yeye
Bush has ears and wall has eyes
Be careful what you say as news travels fast
(and sometimes mysteriously).

44. Buy meat yuh get bone, buy lan yuh get stoane
If you buy meat, you get bones; if you buy land you get stones
There is no perfection in life;
everyone has weaknesses.

45. Brown man wife nyam cackroach ah cawna, sabe money fi buy silk dress
A brown man's wife eats cockroaches in the corner while she saves her money to buy silk dresses
Some people disguise the fact that they are poor by pretending to be rich.

46. Cack mout kill cack
A cock's mouth will kill him
If you talk too much, your own words will condemn you.

47. Cackroach nebber so drunk dat im walk inna fowl yard
Cockroach is never so drunk that he walks into a fowl's yard
If you value your life you will keep away from those who threaten to destroy it;
Never put yourself in unnecessary danger.

48. Cackroach noh business inna fowl fight
A cockroach has no business in a fowl fight
Keep out of other people's business.

49. Cap noh fit yuh noh tek ih up
If a cap doesn't fit you leave it alone
Keep out of issues that don't concern you.

50. Cat noh mek no dawg
Cats do not produce dogs
Children are likely to follow in their parents' footsteps.

51. Chair fall dung bench get up
The chair falls down the bench gets up
No one is indispensable.

52. Chicken merry, hawk deh near
A chicken may be merry but a hawk is nearby
You should always be careful, even when you are having fun.

53. Chink nebber run till im si crowd
A bedbug doesn't show itself until it sees a crowd
Your vulnerabilities are often exposed when you least expect it;
Some people tend to behave badly when they have an audience.

54. Chip nebber fly far fram di black
A chip never falls far from the block
People of the same family or background have similar traits;
Children tend to follow the example set by their parents.

55. Cole cyaan kibba cole
Cold cannot cover cold
People with similar weaknesses cannot help each other.
(Similar to: The blind can't lead the blind)

56. Count de caas before yuh mount yuh hawse
Count your cost before you mount your horse
Ensure you understand any venture you are undertaking and plan your actions in advance.

57. Cow noh hab noh business inna hawse-play
Cows have no business in horse-play
People should mind their own business.

58. Cow dat belong ah butcha nebber seh im berry well
A cow that belongs to a butcher never says that she is very well
Sometimes you have to lie to save yourself.

59. Cowad man keep soun bone
A coward man keeps sound bones
While it may be acceptable to be adventurous and take risks, be aware that risktaking is dangerous and you could get hurt.

60. Cow nebba know di use ah im tail till im lose ih
A cow doesn't know the use of its tail until it loses it
You don't appreciate who or what you have until you no longer have them; take nothing for granted.

61. Cow noh dead im wi shake im tail
A cow that is not dead will shake its tail
Never give up on someone while they are still alive.
(Similar to: while there's life there's hope)

62. Cow seh "Tan up noh mean rest
Cow says, "Standing up doesn't mean resting"
Appearances can be deceiving.

63. Crab cyaan hol inna lobster shell
A crab cannot fit into a lobster's shell
Be aware of social barriers.

64. Crab know seh im back noh strong im noh dig ole
Crab says that he knows his back isn't strong so he

doesn't dig a hole
Don't get into situations where you know that you will not be able to bear the consequences.

65. Craben choke puppy
Craven chokes puppy
If you are greedy you will get hurt.

66. Crab seh im noh trus noh shedda afta dawk
The crab says that he doesn't trust any shadow after dark
You have a right to be sceptical when dealing with people who are shady in their dealings.

67. Cry-cry boot noh good fi aise
A squeaking boot is no good for the ears
No one enjoys hearing constant complaints.

68. Cuss-cuss noh bore ole inna mi kin
Curses bore no hole in my skin
Mere words cannot inflict physical pain.

69. Cuss dawg but nebber seh im teeth noh white
You can curse a dog, but never say that its teeth aren't white
Give credit where it is due; don't allow people's faults to rob you of your objectivity.

70. Cuss Jankro peel ed an turkey bex
If you curse a crow about its bald-head a turkey will be vexed
If you offend someone, you also offend his kind and they too become your enemies.

71. Cyaan tan fur trow salt inna pat
You cannot stay far and throw salt in a pot
Don't share sensitive information from a distance; be discreet!

72. Dawg ah sweat but long hair hide ih
A dog is sweating but his long hair hides it
Those with money can afford to hide their weaknesses.

73. Dawg cyaan manage bone im throw ih weh, fowl go pick ih up
When a dog cannot manage a bone it throws it away, yet a fowl goes and picks it up

Part I: Proverbs and Sayings

If the experts cannot handle a situation, don't assume you can!

74. Dawg foot bruk im fine im massa yard
If a dog's foot is broken he finds his master's house
Those who get hurt in life will eventually return home.

75. Dawg-flea tell im pickney im mustn't seh im dead till im ketch pan finger nail
A dog flea told his child that he must not say that he is dead until he is caught on someone's finger nail
Don't write people off as long as they're alive.
(Similar to: While there's life there's hope)

76. Dawg hab four foot but im cyaan walk four different way
A dog has four legs but it cannot walk in four different directions
There is a limit as to what money can do for you; having more of it doesn't mean that you will be more contented.

77. Dawg lib well im trouble cow ah pass
A dog that has a good life bothers cows
Those who can afford not to work will spend their time interfering with others.

78. Dawg nebber fight ova dry bone
Dogs never fight over dry bones
If you are fighting over an issue, make sure it's worth it.

79. Dawg seh if im av money im wouda buy im owna fleas
A dog said that if it had money it would buy its own fleas
When some people have money they waste it on unnecessary things.

80. Dawg wid too much owna go ah bed hungry
Dog with too many owners go to bed without supper
There comes a time when you have to settle down and focus on your goals.
(Similar to: A rolling stone gathers no moss)

81. De bes ah field mus hab weed
Even the best fields have weeds
No-one is perfect.

82. Deble ole but im noh bedridden
The devil is old but not bedridden
People who are wicked when they are young don't change simply because they have grown older.

83. Def eaz gi liad chouble
Deaf ears are a trouble to liars
If you don't listen or if you cannot hear what is being said, you risk misinterpreting it;
Try not to pass on incorrect information.

84. Dere's no disease dat time cyaan cure
There is no disease that time cannot cure
Time is the master; everything will fall into place in due course.

85. Di bigger di fish di more butta ih tek
The bigger the fish the more butter it requires
Don't be overly ambitious; big projects require more resources.

86. Di bud weh sing di bes noh mek di bes nes
The bird that sings the best does not necessarily make the best nest
Those who brag about their ability are not necessarily the best candidates for the job.
(Similar to: Self praise is no recommendation)

87. Di darkes paat ah night ah wen day soon lite
The darkest part of the night is just before dawn
It gets worse before it gets better.

88. Di deeper yuh dig de richer di soil
The deeper you dig, the richer the soil
The greater the effort, the richer the rewards.

89. Di hiya di monkey clime, di more im expose
The higher the monkey climbs the more it is exposed
The higher people climb up the social ladder the more their character is revealed.

90. Di moe yuh lib di moe yuh larn
The longer you live the more you learn
Wisdom increases with age.

Part I: Proverbs and Sayings

Enchanted Gardens (above);

Cranbrook Flower Forest (below)

Jamaican Proverbs and Places and Symbols

Hope Gardens, Kingston and St. Andrew (above)

Emancipation Park, Kingston (below)

Part I: Proverbs and Sayings

North South Highway (above)
Mandela Highway (below)

Jamaican Proverbs and Places and Symbols

Kingston at night (above)

Night in the Finacial District - New Kingson (below)

Part I: Proverbs and Sayings

91. Di man dat hab on boot mus go befoe fi mash macca
The man who is wearing boots must lead the way and trample the thorns.
Those with resources must create opportunities
for those without.

92. Di moe yuh look di less yuh si
The more you look the less you see
Sometimes the information you seek is right in front of you.

93. Di olda de bull di stiffer di horn
The older the bull, the stiffer the horns
The older you get the more assertive
(and perhaps more stubborn) you become.

94. Di olda di clock di fassser ih wine
The older the clock the faster it winds
People become wiser as they grow older.

95. Di olda di moon di bryta ih shine
The older the moon, the brighter it shines
Wisdom increases with age.

96. Di only cure fi sleep ah sleep
The only cure for sleep is sleep
Irrespective of how busy you are you must find time to sleep.

97. Di race ah noh fi di swift nar di battle fi di strong but fi he who persevere to di en
The race is not for the swift or the battle for the strong, but for he who perseveres to the end
Perseverance is key; don't worry about moving at a
fast pace, focus instead on completing.

98. Di wises man ah sometimes fool
The wisest man is sometimes a fool
Everyone has moments of vulnerability.

99. Dirt noh kill nobady unless ih drop pan dem
Dirt doesn't kill anyone unless it falls on them
Don't be afraid to get your hands dirty.

100. Dish claat com tun table towel
A dish-cloth has become a table towel
Some people who are not accustomed to having nice things tend to show off when their fortune changes.

101. Doan count yuh chicken befoe dem hatch
Don't count your chickens before they are hatched
It is not wise to pre-empt an outcome and make plans accordingly.

102. Doan mek yuh lef han know wah yuh right han ah du
Don't allow your left hand to know what your right hand is about
Keep some things to yourself; don't disclose everything even to those nearest and dearest to you.

103. Doan run befoe yuh walk
Don't run before you walk
Take things in stages; don't ignore the early steps.

104. Donkey seh di worl noh level
The donkey says that the world is not level
Some people enjoy an unfair advantage in life; Ups and downs are part of life.

105. Draft steer nebber mek saddle hawse
A draft steer never turns into a saddle horse
Some people are far too crude and rough to ever becoming refined.

106. Drunk man talk di truth
A drunken man speaks the truth
When people are under the influence of alcohol they invariably speak the truth.

107. Dry stump ah cane piece noh fi laugh when cane piece
ketch ah fire
A dry stump in a cane plantation should not laugh when the plantation catches fire
Don't rejoice at other people's demise; you could be more vulnerable than you think!

108. Duck an fowl feed togeda but dem noh roos togeda
Ducks and chickens may feed together but they do not dwell together
People from different social classes may interact out of necessity but don't expect this interaction to go beyond a certain level.

109. Duppy know who fi frighten
Ghosts know whom they should frighten
Bullies know who to pick on;
People will always heckle those they perceive to be weaker.

110. Eat wid di deble but gi'im a long spoon
Eat with the devil but give him a long spoon
You have to associate with all kinds of people but they don't have to become your friends.

111. Ebery cave-hole hab im own duppy
Every cave has its own ghost
Everyone has secrets and everyone faces challenges.

112. Ebery dawg ha im day an ebery puss im four o' clock
Every dog has its day and every cat its four o' clock
Everyone has his time to shine.

113. Ebery dawg tink im ah lian inna im massa yard
Every dog thinks he is a lion in his master's yard
People are more confident and powerful when they are on their own territory.

114. Ebery day ah fishing-day but noh ebery day fi ketch fish
You may go fishing every day, but some days you will not catch any fish at all
Don't always expect your efforts to yield rewards.

115. Every day bucket ah go ah well, one day di battom ah go drap out
Every day the bucket is taken to the well, one day the bottom will drop out
Those who consistently take risks will get caught eventually.

116. Ebery day deble help tief one day God wi help watchman
Every day the devil helps the thief, one day God helps the watchman
People who consistently do wrong will eventually be caught.

117. Ebery danki sing fram im own hymn sheet
Every donkey sings from his own hymn sheet
Every man to his own order;
People protect their own interest.

118. Ebery day yuh ah beat donkey one day im ah go kick yuh
If every day you beat a donkey one day it will kick you
People have a limit as to how much abuse they will tolerate before they retaliate.

119. Ebery fambily av im bruk foot
Every family has its own broken leg
Every family has vulnerable members.

120. Ebery mickle mek a muckle
Every bit adds up
Every little counts.

121. Ebery oe av im tick ah bush
Every hoe has its matching stick in the bush
There is someone for everyone.

122. Ebery pot haffi siddung pan im own batty
Every pot has to sit down on its own bottom
Every man must be responsible for himself!

123. Ebery spwoil mek a style
Every spoil makes a style
Every spoilt situation is an opportunity to be creative.

124. Ebery time rain set jancro seh im ah go mek house
Every time the rain sets the crow says he is going to make a house
Stop procrastinating before it's too late.

Part I: Proverbs and Sayings

Ocho Rios Harbour and Pier (above and below)
St. Ann

Jamaican Proverbs and Places and Symbols

Falmouth Cruise Port, Trelawny (above)
Goblin Island, Portland (below)

Part I: Proverbs and Sayings

Holland Bamboo (above)
Lovers Leap, St. Elizabeth (below)

Blue Lagoon, Portland (above)
Negril Cliffs below (below)
(Photos courtesy of the JTB & Trip Advisor)

125. Ebery tinking fish hab im buyer
Every stinking fish has its buyer
There is someone for everyone.

126. Empty bag cyaan stan up
An empty bag cannot stand up
A hungry worker won't do a good job.

127. Empty barrel mek di mose naize
Empty barrel makes the most noise
People conceal their ignorance by pretending to be very knowledgeable about a subject.

128. Ebery tun yuh tun macca juk yuh
Every time you turn thorns prick your skin
Trials and tribulations abound in life.

129. Eye lash olda dan beard
The eyelash is older than the beard
Show respect to your elders

130. Eye noh si haart noh leap
What the eyes don't see doesn't affect the heartbeat
What you don't know doesn't hurt you.

131. Falla fashan mek monkey lose im tail
A monkey that follows fashion will lose its tail
Don't get into the habit of copying other people's habits.

132. Falla fashan monkey nebber bwoile a good soup yet
A follow fashion monkey has never made a good soup
The copy is never as good as the original.

133. Finger nebber seh "look yah," ih seh "look deh"
A finger never says "look here"; it says "look there"
People don't usually focus on their own faults.

134. Finger tink yuh cyaan cut ih off an trow ih weh
Even If your finger stinks you cannot cut it off and throw it away
Support your friends and family if they are in trouble, irrespective of the mistakes that they may have made.

135. Fire deh ah muss-muss tail, im tink ah cool breeze

Fire is at a mouse' tail it thinks it's cool breeze
You may be heading for trouble and not even realise it.

136. Fish ah deep water noh know ow fish ah rivvaside feel
Fish in deep waters don't know how the fish in shallow waters feel
People who live in a secure environment cannot understand how those who live in dangerous situations feel;
Those who are fortunate enough to be wealthy can never understand the suffering of the poor.

137. Fish-bone noh ladge inna pickney troat alone
Fish bones don't lodge only in children's throats
Misfortune takes no account of age or vulnerability; it strikes anyone.

138. Fool-fool dawg bark at flying bud
A foolish dog barks at a flying bird
Don't waste time pining after someone who has no interest in you or after something that is simply out of your reach.

139. Fool-fool pickney mek fowl get weh from im two time
A foolish child allows a fowl to escape on a second occasion
Only a fool allows himself to be tricked in the same way over and over.

140. Fowl agree fi hatch duck egg but im noh agree fi teach
duck pickney fi swim
A fowl agrees to hatch a ducks egg but doesn't agree to teach the duckling to swim
People will help you to a certain point, after that it's up to you to help yourself.

141. Fowl feed ah han eezy fi ketch
A chicken that's fed by hand is easily caught
Those close to us are easily caught.

142. Fowl nyam done im rub im mout pan grung
A fowl finishes eating then it rubs its mouth on the ground
Some people are particularly ungrateful.

143. Fowl seh im noh business inna mongoose politics
A fowl says that he has no business in mongoose politics
Mind your own business.

144. Fox cyaan ketch di grape im seh ih sour
The fox cannot reach the grape he says its sour
People will speak ill of you if they are unable to get what they want from you.

145. Frog nebber gargle im troat till im tase fresh wahta
A frog never gargle its throat until it tastes fresh water
Some people just love to show off when strangers are around.

146. Frog seh wat is joke to yuh is det to mi
Frog says that what is joke to you is death to him
Don't amuse yourself at another person's expense.

147. Fry di big fish fus di lilly one afta
Fry the big fish first and then the smaller ones
Know what your priorities are.

148. Gi yuh hawse yuh waan saggle
I gave you a horse now you want a saddle
Some people can't be satisfied with what they are given; they always want more.

149. God Almighty know why im bruk fowl wing
God knows why he broke the fowl's wing
Some people are simply too arrogant and have to be humbled.

150. God mek man strait, ah rum mek im fall dung
God made man upright but rum makes him fall to the ground
An individual who is under the influence of alcohol is prone to doing silly things.

151. Good fowl a gaah market sensé fowl pick up demself deh follow back a dem
A good fowl is going to a market, a sensé fowl picks up itself and follows in tow
People of a lower class people will endeavour to associate themselves with those perceived to be higher up the social ladder.

152. Good fren betta dan packit money

A good friend is better than pocket money
Be appreciative of your friends and don't take them for granted.

153. Great good nebber get by likkle pain
A great good is never achieved by little pain
Success does not come easily.

154. Haard aise mek a soft behind
"Hard ears" make a soft bottom
Disobedient children will be duly punished.

155. Haard aise pickney nyam rackstone
"Hard ears" children eat rock stone
Children who disobey their parents will have a hard life.

156. Haard aise pickney walk two time
"Hard ears" children walk twice
Those who insist on being stubborn will suffer unduly.

157. Haard wok noh kill nohbady
Hard work has never killed anyone
Hard work has its rewards.

158. Haard ah hearing pickney ded ah sun hot
A disobedient child dies from the heat of the sun
Children who will not listen to advice will struggle in life.

159. Han go paki come
A hand goes out, a calabash comes in
If you are in the habit of helping others you in turn will receive support.

160. Hase mek wase
Haste makes waste
Too much rush can make you waste your time.

161. Hat needle bun thread
A hot needle burns thread
Harsh behaviour causes missed opportunities; be tactful!

162. High seat kill Miss Thomas puss
It was a high seat that killed Miss Thomas' cat
Being in a high position carries its own risks;
Also literally - sitting on a high seat can be dangerous.

163. Hog run fi im life dawg run fi im character
A pig runs for its life, a dog runs for its character
People don't all have the same values.

164. Hog seh di fus water im ketch im wallah
Pig says that he washes in the first water he finds
Seize the first opportunity that presents itself.

165. Hog seh why yuh mout so lang, mumma seh you ah com you wi si
Hog asked: why is your mouth so long? The mother answered: you are coming, you will see
Though you fail to understand some key lessons when you are young, in time all becomes clear.

166. Hawse noh too good fi carry im own grass
A horse is not too good to carry its own grass
No one is too good to perform acts that may be regarded as lowly, if it is ultimately to his/her benefit.

167. Howdy an tenk yuh noh bruk noh square
"Hello" and "thank you" do not break any squares
Greeting and thanking people do not require a lot of effort.

168. Humble calf suck di most milk
A humble calf sucks the most milk
You will get more cooperation from someone if you are nice to them.

169. Hungry belly an full belly noh walk ah pass
A hungry belly and a full belly don't share the same path
Those with money cannot comprehend the misery of those without.

170. Hungry dawg nyam roas kaarn
A hungry dog will eat roast corn
Desperate situations demand desperate measures.

171. Hungry fowl wake soon
A fowl that is hungry wakes early
Those with basic needs, must be proactive in finding ways to satisfy them

172. Idle dawg worry sheep
An idle dog bothers sheep
Those who have nothing to do will waste their time doing silly things.

173. Idle man head ah deble workshop
The head of an idle person is a workshop for the devil
The devil finds work for idle hands.

174. Idle man tempt di deble
An idle man tempts the devil
People with nothing to do ultimately get into trouble.

175. If ah noh soh ah neally soh
If it's not like that, it is nearly that
There is often some truth in stories you hear on the grapevine.

176. If bees nebber hab sting im woulden keep im honey
If bees did not have sting, they wouldn't be able to keep their honey
People have a right to protect their property, even if they are perceived as being mean.

177. If cow ben know ow im troat hole tan him wouden chance pear seed
If a cow had known how his throat was he wouldn't have attempted to eat an avocado seed
We should acknowledge our limitations and operate accordingly.

178. If dere was no fool cunnyman couldn lib
If there were no fools, conmen couldn't live
Don't allow yourself to be fooled.

179. If danki bray afta yuh noh bray afta im
If a donkey brays at you, you shouldn't attempt to bray at the donkey
It takes two to quarrel; avoid confrontations by keeping your mouth shut.

180. If fish coulda keep im mouth shut im woulda nebber get caught
If fish had kept its mouth shut it would never have got caught
Mind your own business and keep out of trouble.

181. If fool noh go ah market bad sinting noh sell
If fools don't go to market, foolishness wouldn't sell
Don't complain about the bad purchases you made; spend your money wisely!

182. Ih haad fi get butta outta dawg troat
It is difficult to take butter out of a dog's throat
It is hard to get anything from miserly people.

183. Ih haad fi keep out di debil but ih wos fi drive im out
It is difficult to keep out the devil but even more difficult to drive him out.
It is hard to keep out of trouble but harder still to get out once you are involved.

184. If new oe waan fi know ow grung tough mek im ax ole oe
If a new hoe wants to know how tough the ground is, he should ask an old hoe
Don't be afraid to ask more experienced people for advice.

185. If plantn ben know seh im neck woudda bruk im wouldda nebber shoot
Had the plantain known that its neck would be broken it would never have borne fruit
People should avoid venturing into territory that will ultimately bring their downfall.

186. If wind noh blow fowl batty noh show
If the wind doesn't blow a fowl's bottom isn't exposed
It's only in a crisis that you can see people's true character.

187. If yuh back monkey im wi fight tiga
If you support a monkey it will fight a tiger
Support and encouragement boost people's confidence and they will embrace bigger and more rewarding challenges.

188. If yuh barn fi heng yuh cyaan drown
If you are born to be hanged you cannot drown
Every man has his own destiny.

189. If yuh fly wid jankro yuh nyam rotten meat
If you fly with vultures you will eat rotten meat

If you associate with obnoxious people you will
soon become like them.
(Similar to: Show me your friends and I'll tell you who you are)

190. If yuh call tiga massa ih wi nyam yuh
If you call the tiger a master, it will devour you
If you are too humble people will trample you.

191. If yuh crape gourdy yuh fine worm-ole
If you scrape a gourdy you will find worm holes
If you search for faults you will find them.

192. If yuh cyaan bear di name noh play de game
If you cannot bear the name don't play the game
If you don't want to be blamed, keep away from shady deals;
If you cannot bear the consequences, avoid the situation entirely.

193. If yuh cyaan find callalu tek junjo
If you can't find callalloo, use moss
If you can't have exactly what you want, use what's available.

194. If yuh cyaan hear yuh wi feel
If you cannot hear you will feel
Failure to heed advice could lead to dire consequences.

195. If yuh cyaan ketch quako yuh ketch im shut
If you can't catch the bird, catch its young
If you cannot catch your target, then try holding on to the
person nearest and dearest to him.

196. If yuh cyaan tek di heat get outta di kitchen
If you cannot take the heat, get out of the kitchen
If you cannot take the pressure of a particular situation,
find an alternative.

197. If yuh fallaw wah rivva carry yuh nebber drink di wahta
*If you were aware of all that lies in the river you would
never drink the water*
If you were aware of the true character of some people
you would avoid them at all costs.

Part I: Proverbs and Sayings

Portmore Plaza, St. Catherine (above)
Emancipation Square, Spanish Town (below)

Jamaican Proverbs and Places and Symbols

Montego Bay Resort Centre (above)
Harmony Hill Great House, Mo-Bay (below)
(Photos courtesy of The JTB)

Part I: Proverbs and Sayings

Goblin Hill (above)
Monkey Island/Pellew Island (below)
Portland

Jamaican Proverbs and Places and Symbols

Sandals Royal Caribbean's overwater bungalows, Montego Bay
(above)
Love Bridge Negril (below)
(Photos courtesy of the Jamaican Observer and Trip Advisor)

198. If yuh get hol ah di blade mine how yuh draw
If you are holding the blade be careful how you draw
If you are at a disadvantage, consider retreating.

199. If yuh get spoon yuh wi drink soup
If you get a spoon chances are you will drink soup
People will excel if they have the right tools and are given an opportunity.

200. If yuh go ah tump-a-foot dance yuh mus dance tump-a-foot
If you go to "tump-a-foot" dance you must dance "tumpa-a-foot"
When in Rome do as the Romans.

201. If yuh hab dawg fi bark fi yuh, yuh noh need fi bark
If you have a dog to bark for you there is no need for you to bark
If you have people to work for you, what's the point of doing it yourself?
Those who can afford to engage manpower will do so.

202. If yuh hea di deble ah come clear di way
If you hear the devil coming, clear the way
Keep out of trouble's way.

203. If yuh lib wid dawg yuh larn fi bark
If you live with a dog you'll learn to bark
You are influenced by those with whom you associate.
(Similar to: Show me your friends and I will tell you who you are)

204. If yuh lie wid dawg yuh wi rise wid fleas
If you lie with a dog you are certain to rise with fleas
It is easy to assume the bad habits of those with whom we keep company.

205. If yuh lie yuh wi tief
If you lie you will steal
Lying and stealing go together; never trust a liar!

206. If yuh lob licky-licky pot wi bun yuh finga
If you love pickings, your fingers will get burnt
Be cautious of gifts and bribes; they could land you in trouble.

207. If yuh mek yuh bed hard yuh lie on it hard

If you make your bed hard you lie on it hard
If you make wrong decisions be prepared to endure the consequences.

208. If yuh cyaan walk fast tek time run
If you cannot walk fast run slowly
If you can't find an absolute solution, consider taking the next best option.

209. If yuh noh go unda fowl roost fowl cyaan shit pon yuh
If you don't go under a fowl roost, fowls won't be able to defecate on you
Keep away from trouble and you won't be blamed for anything that happens.

210. If yuh noh done nyam noh dash weh yuh plate
If you haven't finished eating, don't discard your plate
Don't celebrate prematurely; it is not over until it is truly over.

211. If yuh noh hab good fi seh noh seh nuttn
If you have nothing good to say don't say anything
It's better not to say anything than to speak negatively about people.

212. If yuh noh waah leaf drop pan yuh tan fram unda di tree
If you don't want leaf to drop on you don't go under the tree
Avoid situations that can have undesirable consequence or in which you can be blamed.

213. If yuh nyam egg yuh mus bruk di shell fuss
If you eat eggs you must break the shell first
You will encounter and must overcome challenges if you expect to achieve great things.

214. If yuh play wid fire yuh wi get bun
If you play with fire you will get burnt
If you continuously involve yourself in dangerous situations you will eventually get hurt.

215. If yuh run too fast yuh wi pass yuh place
If you run too fast you will pass your place

If you do things in a hurry you'll make costly mistakes; it's better for you to plan and pace yourself.

216. If yuh spit in di sky ih will fall in yuh eye
If you spit in the sky it will fall in your eye
If you ill-treat people, in due course you in turn will be ill-treated; show gratitude!

217. If yuh tan ah market lang yuh wi owe debt
If you spend a long time in the market you will become indebted
Manage your money wisely and avoid the temptation to overspend.

218. If yuh throw stoane in a hog pen di one weh bawl out ah im get di lick
If you throw stone in a pigsty, the one that cries out is the one that was hit
People are who they reveal themselves to be, not who we think they are.

219. If yuh trousers too short wear long braces
If your trousers are too short, wear long braces
Be aware of your shortcomings and make provisions for them.

220. If you waah fi know if mawga dawg av teeth draw im tail
If you want to know if a meagre dog has teeth, tug at its tail
Don't be tempted to interfere with peaceful people or you will be surprised by their wrath.

221. If yuh waah fi ride far spare di hawse
If you want to ride far, spare the horse
Treat people with respect and they will go the extra mile for you.

222. If yuh waah half a bread beg smaddy buy ih but if yuh waah wan buy ih yuself
If you want half of a loaf, ask someone to buy it; but if you want a whole bread go and buy it yourself
If you want something to be done properly, do it yourself.

223. If yuh waah good yuh nose haffi run
If you want good your nose must run
You have to work hard for what you want.

224. If yuh doan mash ants yuh doan fine im gut
If you don't mash an ant, you won't find its gut
People's true personality emerges when you have a dispute with them.

225. If yuh waah fi know yuh fren lay down ah roadside farm drunk
If you want to know who your friends are, lay down by the roadside and pretend to be drunk
Your true friends don't acknowledge you only in the good times; they stick by you when the chips are down.
(Similar to: A friend in need is a friend indeed)

226. If yuh waah milk feed di goat
If you want milk, feed the goat
You have got to put something in if you want to get something out.
(Similar to: Encouragement sweetens labour)

227. In de lang run di cheapes ah di deares
In the long run the cheapest is the dearest
What appears to be the cheapest can cost considerably more in the long term.

228. In ebery poun ah lie dere is a ounce ah truth
In every pound of lie there is an ounce of truth
There is usually some degree of truth, however minute, in gossip; If you examine a negative situation closely, you will find something positive.

229. It betta fi lose yuh time dan yuh character
It is better to lose your time than to lose your character
Protect your integrity at all costs.

230. Jankro seh im cyaan wok pon Sunday
Crow says that he cannot work on Sundays
People cannot be forced to work on public holidays if they really don't want to do so.

231. Jankro waan go a Louan im get cool breeze im fly faster
If a crow is going to Louan he will fly faster if he gets cool breeze
People will work harder if they are encouraged and supported.
(Similar to: Encouragement sweetens labour)

232. Jump outta frying pan an inna di fire
Jump out of frying pan and into the fire
Be careful that you are not leaving a bad situation for a similar or worse one.

233. Kick dawg im fren yuh, feed im im bite yuh
If you kick a dog he will befriend you but if you feed him he will bite you
Some people respond better to bad treatment.

234. Kiss ass befoe yuh lick ih
Kiss an arse before you slap it
In order to appeal to someone, you need to be humble but once you have what you want you no longer have to grovel.

235. Kunnu no hab good bottam im cyaan go ah sea
If a canoe does not have a good bottom it cannot go to the sea
People must ensure that their foundation is sound before they build on it.

236. Laffi laffi easy fi lie dung
He who laughs a lot is easy to lie down
Take life seriously or you may be used or abused by others who will make wrong assumptions about your character.

237. Lawya look pan yuh wid one yeye but im look pan yuh packet wid two
A lawyer looks at you with one eye but uses both eyes to inspect your pocket
Some people have no time for you but will find the time if they feel that they can benefit financially.

238. Lass pickney kill mumma
The last child kills his mother
There is a limit to everything – the last straw breaks the camel's back.

239. Larn fi dance ah yaad befoe yuh dance abroad
Learn to dance at home before you dance abroad
Hone your skills at home before showing them off in public.

240. Likkle axe cut dung big tree

A small axe can be used to fall a big tree
Size doesn't matter it's the effect that counts;
Never underestimate people's potential!

241. Likkle bit ah ram goat ave beard an big bull noh av nun
A little ram goat may have a beard whereas a big bull has none
Younger people or those smaller in stature often have great attributes that are lacking in more mature people or those of a larger frame.

242. Likkle bud cyaa seeds very far
Little birds carry seeds very far
Be careful what you say in the presence of little children, they are good at bearing tales.

243. Likkle wabba av big aise
Little warblers have big ears
Be careful what you say in the presence of children.

244. Lilly kunue tan near di shore
A little canoe stays near the shore
People must understand their capabilities and not put themselves in undue danger.

245. Lizard nebber know weh im deh till im fine himself inna puss mout
A lizard never knows where he is until he finds himself in a cat's mouth
People often realise that they are in trouble only when it's too late.

246. Lizard noh fraid fi walk ah road late because im noh good fi nyam
Lizards are not edible so they are not afraid to walk on the streets late at night
People with nothing to lose will take more risks.

247. Lang road draw sweat short cut draw blood
Long road draws sweat short cut draws blood
The shortest route is not always the best one;
Although the longer route can be tiring, it is often the better choice.

248. Man ah sea noh know how man ah lan feel
A man at sea doesn't know how a man ashore feels
Wealthy people do not truly comprehend the suffering of the poor.

249. Man hab cow im look fi milk
A man with cow looks for milk
People base their expectations on their personal circumstances.

250. Man dat carry straw noh fi fool wid fire
Someone who carries straw shouldn't play with fire
Those who are vulnerable in certain situations should exercise caution. (If you live in a glass house, don't throw stones)

251. Man av raw meat im look fi fire
A man who has raw meat looks for a fire
If you have problems, proactively look for solutions; don't expet them to be sorted by someone else.

252. Man belly full im seh anyting
When a man's belly is full he will say anything
Those who have money can say whatever they want to say.

253. Man nebber know de use ah water till di tank run dry
A man never knows the use of water until the tank runs dry
People often do not appreciate others until they no longer have access to them.

254. Man noh dead noh call im duppy
If a man is not dead, don't call him a ghost
As long as someone is alive, don't dismiss their potential/ don't write them off.

255. Man noh hab goudy im satisfy wid bottle
A man who doesn't have a calabash is satisfied with a bottle
Be grateful for the little that you have, though you may yearn for more.

256. Man no pread clothes ah doah im noh watch rain
If a man has not spread out his clothes to dry he does not watch the rain
If you have nothing to lose you won't be unduly concerned about threats.

257. Man sleep inna fowl nes but fowl nes ah noh im bed
A man sleeps in a nest but a nest is not his bed
People devise short term solutions to their problems,
but that doesn't change the fact that
they have aspirations.

258. Man weh shit a pass noh memba, ah di one weh clean ih
*The man who defecates on the road doesn't remember
it but the one who cleans it does*
The person who has done wrong never remembers,
but the one who has been wronged never forgets it.

259. Mannas tek yuh thru di worl
Having manners will take you throughout the world
There are benefits to be derived from having good manners.

260. Man widout wife like a kitchen widout a knife
A man without a wife is like a kitchen without a knife
People need companionship.

261. Mangoose seh man who cyaan tek risk ah noh man at all
The mongoose says that a man who can't take risks is not a man
Taking risks is a life skill; it promotes maturity.

262. Many ways to heng a dawg without putting rope roun im neck
*There are many ways to hang a dog without putting
a rope around its neck*
There are many strategies that can be used to get even with
someone.

263. Masquita go ah village fi syrup but im noh always get weh im go fah
*A mosquito goes to the village for syrup but it doesn't
always get what it goes for*
Sometimes you won't get what you want and you have to settle
for less.

264. Me noh call yuh noh come
If I don't call you please don't come
Don't go where you are not welcome.

Part I: Proverbs and Sayings

Mayfield Falls, Westmoreland (above)
Picture courtesy of Trip Advisor
Somerset Falls, Portland (below)

Jamaican Proverbs and Places and Symbols

Dunns River Falls, St. Ann (above)
YS Falls, St. Elizabeth (below)
Pictures courtesy of Trip Advisor & VisitJamaica

Part I: Proverbs and Sayings

Reach Falls, Portland (above)
Sturge Town River, St. Ann (above)

Jamaican Proverbs and Places and Symbols

Irie River, St. Ann (above)
Marthae Brae River, Falmouth
Pictures courtesy of Trip Advisor

Part I: Proverbs and Sayings

265. Mek a fren when yuh noh need one
Make friends even when you don't need them
Don't wait until you need favours from people before you seek to build relationships with them.

266. Mi throw mi corn mi noh call no fowl
I throw my corn I called no fowls
A guilty conscience will feel the target of a general comment even if it was never intended for them.

267. Mischief com by di poun an go by di ounce
Mischief comes in pounds but leaves in ounces
Getting into trouble is easy but getting out of it is painstakingly slow.

268. Money noh bear pon tree
Money doesn't grow on trees
You have to work if you want to achieve prosperity.

269. Monkey deh hide but im tail heng ah doah
A monkey is hiding but his tail is exposed
Some people do all they can to conceal their activities or possessions not realising that others are fully aware of them.

270. Monkey mus know weh im gwine put im tail before im order trousiz
A monkey must know where it is going to put its tail before it orders its trousers
Put plans in place before making important decisions.

271. Monkey play di figgle mek baboon dance
A monkey plays the fiddle for the baboon to dance
Some people just wait for someone to take the lead before they start to make a fool of themselves.
(Similar to: One fool makes many)

272. Monkey si monkey do
What a monkey sees it will copy
People are social beings that enjoy copying the actions of others.

273. Neally nebber kill di bud
Nearly never kills the bird
Complete whatever you start!

274. Nanny-goat nebber cratch im back till im si wall
A nanny goat never scratches its back until it sees a wall
Look out for opportunities and take them when they arise.

275. Nebber squeeze ah dawg tail fi si if im ah sleep
Never squeeze a dog's tail to ascertain whether it is asleep
Avoid stirring up trouble by upsetting harmless people.

276. New broom sweep clean but ole broom know corner
A new broom sweeps clean but an old broom knows the corners
Don't ignore your old friends when new ones appear.

277. Naizy rivva noh drown nobady
A noisy river doesn't drown anyone
Argumentative people are harmless in reality.

278. Noh all foot inna boot ah good foot
Not all feet in boots are good feet
Appearances can be deceiving.

279. Noh ax hungry duck fi watch kaan
Don't ask a hungry duck to watch corn
Don't put temptations in people's way.

280. Noh bill bush fi monkey fi run race
Don't clear the bushes for monkey to run races
Don't waste your time engaging in useless work.

281. Noh bite aff more dan yuh can chew
Don't bite more than you are able to chew
Don't overextend yourself unnecessarily; know your limits.

282. Noh buy cow if yuh can get free milk
There is no need to buy a cow if you can obtain milk, free of charge
Why pay for something if you can have it free of cost.

283. Noh buy puss inna bag
Don't buy a cat in a bag
Sample your goods before you buy them.

284. Noh count ten toe in front ah man wid nine toe
Don't count your ten toes in the presence of a man who has nine toes
Be sensitive to other people's weaknesses; act with discretion.

285. Noh cup noh bruk noh cafee noh dash weh
No cup has been broken no coffee has been spilled
Even when there is a conviction that there is no hope, there is always a possibility that situations can change for the better.

286. Noh cuss alligetta long mout till yuh crass di river
Don't curse an alligator about his long mouth until you cross the river
Don't curse those blocking your way, at least until you have passed them.

287. Noh dash weh yuh tick till yuh crass di river
Don't throw away your stick until you cross the river
Don't celebrate prematurely; it is not over until the race is won.

288. Noh drive fly fram anodda man cow kin
Don't drive away flies from another man's cowskin
Mind your own business and leave other people's alone.

289. Noh eat food when ih hat
Don't eat your food when it's hot
Allow situations to settle before attempting to address them; never do so when tempers are flaring.

290. Noh ebery man breakfast ready di same time
Not every man's breakfast is ready at the same time
People grow at different pace and achieve their goals at different moments in their lives.

291. Noh fling stoane behine yuh
Do not throw stones behind you
Be aware of, and remember your roots.

292. Noh heng yuh basket weh yuh han cyaan reach it
Never hang your basket where you cannot reach it
Do not live beyond your means.

293. Noh heng all yuh clothes pon one nail
Don't hang all your clothes on a single nail
Always have a contingency plan.
(Similar to: Don't put all your eggs in one basket)

294. Noh ketchie noh habie
If you don't catch it you won't have it
If you want to have something you have to work for it.

295. Noh matta ow high jankro fly im haffi cum dung
It doesn't matter how high a crow flies, it has to come down
People at the top must be aware that one day they could find themselves at the bottom.

296. No money, no fren
No money, no friends
When you have no money no one wants to be your friend.

297. Noh mek nobady know yuh last wod
Don't allow anyone to know your last word
Don't let people know your thoughts and plans and don't disclose everything you know.

298. Noh mek one donkey choke yuh
Don't allow one donkey to choke you
Don't allow yourself to be misled by a fool.

299. Noh mek yuh sail too big fi yuh ship
Do not make your sail too big for your ship
Don't engage in activities merely to show off when in effect you are unable to sustain them; be aware of your limitations.

300. "Noh mine" mek ship run ashore
"Don't mind" causes ships to run aground
Avoid being passive, get off the fence and have a point of view!
A careless/indifferent attitude doesn't help any situation.

301. Noh care how boar hog try fi hide under sheep wool im grunt always betray im
No matter how a boar pig tries to hide under sheep wool his grunt always betrays him
No matter how much a person tries to disguise himself, the true character will eventually shine through.

302. Noh put yuself inna barrel when match box can hole yuh
Don't put yourself into a barrel when a match box can hold you
Don't pretend to be someone (more accomplished) than you are not.

303. Noh wait till drum beat before yuh grine yuh axe
Do not wait until the drum beats before you grind your axe
Always be prepared.

304. Noh fatten cackroach fi fowl
Don't fatten cockroach for fowl
Beware of ungrateful people.

305. Noh gi rat cheese fi carry
Don't give a rat cheese to carry
Don't put temptation in the way of needy or greedy people.

306. Noh swap black dawg fi monkey
Don't swap a black dog for a monkey
Be careful not to exchange one bad situation for another.

307. Noh trubble trubble till trubble tek yuh
Don't interfere with trouble until trouble takes you
Steer clear of trouble but defend yourself if necessary.

308. Noh waste powda pan black bud
Don't waste powder on black birds
Don't waste your resources on people who are bent in their own ways - old habits die hard.

309. Nuff bone ah dungle come fram good man table
Many bones in the dung heap came from good men's tables
Many seemingly worthless people come from good families.

310. Nutten nebber happen befoe di time
Nothing happens before the time
There is a time for everything.

311. Ole ooman ah swear fi nyam callalu, callalu ah swear fi wok ol ooman belly
An old woman is swearing for callaloo while the callaloo is swearing for the old woman
You may be planning for someone but be warned,

they may be planning for you too.

312. Ole ooman half ah hoe bring new one
An old woman's half a hoe brings a new one
Be careful when using other people's faulty items
as you may have to replace them.

313. Old fiah-tick easy fi lite
An old fire-stick is easy to light
An old flame (former lover) can easily re-enter your life.

314. Once bitten twice shy
If you are bitten once you will be shy the next time
If you have been adversely affected by a particular situation,
you will exercise caution in future.

315. One bite cyaan nyam mango
One bite cannot eat a mango
You must be thorough in whatever you do;
taking short cuts is not advisable.

316. One han wash di other
One hand washes the other
Try to help others while you can, there will come
a time when you too will need assistance.

317. One hand cyaan clap
One hand cannot clap
We need to support each other; it is difficult for people
to be successful without some degree of assistance.

318. One man beat di bush an annoda one ketch di bud
One man beats the bush and another one catches the bird
He who puts in the hard work is often denied a share
of the spoils;
People work in harmony in order to achieve success.

319. One-one cocoa full basket
One by one, each cocoa helps to fill a basket
Every little bit counts; don't disregard small amounts.

320. One yeye man ah king inna bline man country
A one-eyed man is a king in a blind man's country

Part I: Proverbs and Sayings

People will hold you in high esteem if they feel that you are better than them in some way.

321. Only shoe know ef stockin hab ole
Only shoes know if there is a hole in the stocking
Only those who are close enough to you know your weaknesses.

322. Orange yellah but yuh noh know ef ih sweet
The orange is yellow but you don't know if it's sweet
Don't judge by appearances.
(Similar to: Don't judge a book by its cover)

323. Parson cyaan preach wid dutty collar cause all yeye deh pon im
A pastor cannot preach with a dirty collar because all eyes are on him
If you are in a position of moral authority, you must lead by example.

324. Parson christen im pickney fus
A pastor christens his child first
People look after their own interests first.

325. Patience an sweet talk mek monkey mate wid puss
Patience and sweet talk lets a monkey mate with a cat
Diplomacy allows you to open doors; be tactful!

326. Patient man ride danki
A patient man rides the donkey
With patience you can overcome even the most stubborn challenge.

327. Peacock hide im foot wen im ear bout im tail
A peacock hides its foot when it hears about its tail
A proud person will take extreme measures in order to hide his weaknesses.

328. Peppa bun hot but ih good fi curry
Pepper burns a lot but it is good for curry
Some circumstances, although painful, will yield benefits in the longer term.

329. Pickney suck dem mumma wen dem young an dem puppa wen dem ole
Children suck their mothers when they are young and their fathers when they get older
Children rely on their mothers when they are young but are a drain on their father's resources as they grow older.

330. Platn ripe cyaan green agaen
Once a plantain is ripe it cannot go back to green
Once innocence is lost it can never be regained.

331. Plat'n waan ded ih go ah hillside go shoot
If a plantain tree wants to die it goes to a hillside to bear
If you insist on courting danger it will find you.

332. Play wid big dawg big dawg bite yuh
If you play with a big dog it will bite you
Associating with people of higher social standing or who have significantly more resources can be painful for those who cannot compete.

333. Play wid puppy, puppy lick yuh mouth
If you play with a puppy it will lick your mouth
If you socialise with ignorant people, they will eventually disrespect you.
(Similar to: Familiarity breeds contempt)

334. Poah man pickney walk one-one, rich man pickney walk gang-gang
A poor man's child walks alone while a rich man's child is well accompanied
Those with money have many friends while for those without, it is a lonely road.

335. Man poah im wod poah
If a man is poor his word is poor
Those without money are powerless.

336. Pot ah cuss kettle seh im battam black
A pot is cursing a kettle by saying its bottom is black
There is no point in being unkind to someone who has vulnerabilities similar to yours.

Part I: Proverbs and Sayings

337. Pound ah fret cyaan pay ounce ah debt
One pound of fretting cannot repay one ounce of debt
Problems are not solved by worrying; the time spent fretting could be more gainfully spent working on solutions.

338. Pretty rose got macca jook
Pretty roses have thorns
There is always a down side to a seemingly perfect situation.

339. Promise is a comfort to a fool
A promise is a comfort to a fool
Don't rely on a promise; always have a contingency plan!

340. Provocation mek dummy man talk
Provocations make a dumb man speak
When people are in trouble or faced with challenges they are forced to be more creative.

341. Pudden cyaan bake widout fiah
You cannot bake a pudding without fire
Before assuming a task, ensure that you have the appropriate tools/resources.

342. Puss belly full rat batty tink
When a cat's belly is full, a rat's bottom is stink
When people don't want something they are prone to finding faults (which are often non-existent).

343. Puss gone rat tek charge
When the cat's away, the mouse takes over
When those in authority are absent, those left behind will do as they please.
(Similar to: When the cat's away the mice will play)

344. Puss an dawg noh av di same luck!
A cat and a dog do not have the same luck
Favouritism will impact on outcomes;
What will work for some people will not work for others.

345. Puss noh hab han but im tek im foot wipe im face
A cat doesn't have hands but it uses its foot to wipe its face
If you don't have the right tools/resources, be creative with what you do have!

346. Rain ah fall but dutty tough
It is raining but the dirt is still tough
Some people live in extreme poverty while there is prosperity all around.
Income is coming in but not enough to meet your needs.

347. Rain doan fall fram di bottom up
The rain doesn't fall from the bottom upwards
Those at the top must start and those below will follow;
People at the top must set example for those below.

348. Rain noh fall ah one man door
It doesn't rain at one man's door only
No one has all the luck.

349. Rat belly full potato av kin
When a rat's belly is full, potato has skin
When you're not in need, you can afford to be unduly selective.

350. Ride an whisle
Ride and whistle
Don't procrastinate when you have work to do; learn to multitask too.

351. Rotten wood cyaan mek furniture
Rotten wood cannot be used to make furniture
Something bad cannot produce something that is good.

352. Sabe money an money wi sabe yuh
Save money and money will save you
Save for your future; don't spend all you have.

353. Saltfish siddong pon de counter ah wait fi bread an butter
Saltfish sits at the counter waiting for bread and butter
Those who are lazy will sit idly by, waiting for something to happen.

354. Same knife stick sheep stick goat
The same knife that sticks a sheep will stick a goat
Whatever someone does to another he can also do to you.

Part I: Proverbs and Sayings

Flat Bridge, Rio Cobre, St. Catherine (above);
Rafting on the Rio Grande, Portland (below)

Mangrove Avenue (above)
Crocodile at Black River Safari, St Elizabeth (below)
Photos courtesy of the JTB

Part I: Proverbs and Sayings

Mystic Mountain, Ocho Rios (above)
Green Grotto Caves, Runaway Bay (below)
Photos Courtesy of JTB

Jamaican Proverbs and Places and Symbols

The many moods of the Jamaican sky

Part I: Proverbs and Sayings

355. Sarry fi poah ting, poah ting kill yuh
Sorry for Poor Thing, Poor Thing kills you
Sometimes you help someone and they hurt you in return.

356. Scawnful dawg nyam dutty pudden
A scornful dog eats dirty pudding
Too much pride can lead to humiliation.
(Similar to: Pride goes before a fall)

357. Scratch ole ooman bak an shi wi mek yuh tase ar peppapot
Scratch the back of an old woman and she will allow you to taste her pepper-pot
Be kind and you will receive kindness.
(Similar to: One good deed deserves another)

358. See an bline hear an deaf
See and blind hear and deaf
Mind your own business.

359. Sensé fowl noh waah fedder but im waah carn
Sensé fowl doesn't want feathers, it wants corn
Don't assume you know what is good for other people; Appearances cannot always be interpreted literally.

360. Sick no kya docta wosser
If the sick doesn't care, the doctor doesn't either
If you don't care about your problems, others won't care about them either.

361. Silent rivva run deep
A silent river runs deep
"Quiet" people are not necessarily quiet; there is often a lot more to them than meets the eye.

362. Si mi an com lib wid mi ah two different ting
To see me and to come and live with me are two different things
You never truly know someone until you have actually had close interaction or actually share a residence with them.

363. Snake seh if im no hol up im head ooman tek im tie wood

*The snake said that if he doesn't hold up its head a
woman will use him to tie wood*
If you are lazy you will be vulnerable to abuse by others;
have ambition!

364. Snake weh waah fi grow up stay inna im ole
A snake that wants to grow up remains in its hole
People should stay within their social circles until they have learnt
key lessons of life in order to cope in the wider society.

365. Some people know yuh wen ah moonshine but ah dark nite dem shake dem fiah-tick inna yuh feace
*Some people know you when the moon is shining
but when the night is dark they shake their fire-sticks in your face*
People want to associate with you are prospering but
pretend they don't know you during the hard times.

366. Sometime you haffi walk roun barricade
Sometimes you have to walk around a barricade
Creative thinking enabales you to circumvent obstacles
You encounter in life.

367. Sorry fi mawga dawg, mawga dog tun roun bite yuh
You have pity on a meagre dog but he in turn bites you
People can be ungrateful.

368. Speak wen spoken to, ansa wen called
Speak when you are spoken to, answer when you are called
Do not interfere into other people's business if it does not concern
you.

369. Spida an fly cyaan mek bargin
Spiders and flies cannot make bargains
It is difficult to be friends with someone whom you cannot trust.

370. Stoane ah rivva battam noh know sun hat
A stone at the bottom of a river doesn't know the heat of the sun
If you are always sheltered and protected it will be difficult
for you to comprehend the concept of hardship.

371. Stranja noh walk ah back door
Strangers do not walk at the back door

Only your friends can hurt you; your enemies cannot get near enough.

372. Strong man build pass mek weak man walk
A strong man clears the path for the weak man to use
Those who are strong have a duty to help those who are weak.

373. Sweep yuh own doah befoe yuh see fi mi
Sweep your own doorway before noticing mine
Sort out your own life before criticising or attacking other people.

374. Sweet wood blaze but im noh keep fire
A sweet wood blazes but doesn't keep fire
A man of good character may express his anger, but he bears no grudge thereafter.

375. Talk an tase yuh tongue
Talk and taste your tongue
Think before you speak.

376. Tan an see noh pwoil noh dance
Stay and look don't cause any trouble
Look but don't touch.

377. Tan fur si betta
Stay far and get a better view
It is often better to observe some situations from a distance rather than actually getting involved in it.

378. Tan pan crooked an cut strait
Stay on crooked and cut straight
Make the best of your current situation until you can do better.

379. Tedeh fi mi tomorrow fi yuh
Today for me tomorrow for you
No-one has all the luck (your turn will come).

80. Tek one stoane kill two bud
Kill two birds with one stone
Plan your time carefully and optimise the opportunities presented to you.

381. Tek sleep mark det
Use sleep to mark death
Learn from your experiences and don't make the same mistake twice.

382. Tek wah yuh get til yuh get wah yuh want
Take what you get until you get what you want
Appreciate what you have until you are able to obtain what you want.

383. Those who cyaan dance seh di music noh good
Those who don't know how to dance say the music is no good
People will find faults and make excuses if they find that they are unable to cope in a situation.

384. Tief noh love fi si tief carry lang bag
A thief doesn't like to see another thief carry a long bag
A dishonest person doesn't like to see his peers flourishing.

385. Time langa dan rope
Time is longer than rope
Be patient; time is the master
(Similar to: There is no disease that time cannot cure).

386. Too much ah one ting good fi nutting
Too much of the same thing is good for nothing
Avoid excessive behaviour, strive for moderation instead.

387. Too many rat nebber dig a good hole
Too many rats never dig a good hole
An oversupply of manpower for a task will adversely affect the outcome.

388. Too much callaloo mek peppa-pot stew bitter
Too much callaloo in a peppa-pot soup makes it taste bitter
Too much of a good thing can spoil everything.

389. Tom drunk but Tom noh fool
Tom may be drunk but Tom is no fool
Appearances can be deceiving.

390. Tree grow come catch tree an grow pass tree to
A tree grows and catches up with other trees and then

Part I: Proverbs and Sayings

outgrows them
Even though you may be at a disadvantage initially, you can become more successful than others who have had a head-start.

391. Tree look soun but woodpecker know wah fi du wid ih
A tree may appear sound but a woodpecker knows what to do with it
No matter how powerful you may be there is always someone who can identify and exploit your vulnerability.

392. Trousiz too big fe hawse dawg seh gimme ya
A pair of trousers is too big for a horse, a dog says "give it to me"
People must recognise their limitations; there's no point assuming responsibilities where those more equipped and more capable have failed.

393. Trubble deh a bush Anancy bring ih come ah yaad
There's trouble in the bush Anancy brings it home
Be careful not to invite trouble into your life by trying too hard to help someone.

394. Trubble mek big man wear pickney shut
When in trouble a grown man will wear a child's shirt
When in trouble people will take unconventional and creative actions to get out.

395. Trubble mek de man money mek di manstah
Trouble makes the man, money makes the monster
Challenges build people's character but the love of money destroys it.

396. Trubble mek puss run up prickly pear
Trouble makes a cat run up a prickly pear plant
When people are in trouble they are more likely to take risks.

397. Trubble noh set like rain
Trouble doesn't announce its coming like the rain does
You don't always see trouble looming; it often just happens; be careful!

398. Tun yuh han an mek fashan
Turn your hand and make fashion

Make the best use of scarce resources; be creative!

399. Two bull cyaan reign inna one pen
Two bulls cannot live in one pen
Two leaders can't rule in the same place.

400. Two head betta dan one even if one ah cocoa head
Two heads are better than one even if one is a cocoa head
It is good to work together even if some individuals
are weaker than others.

401. Two jackass cyaan bray ah di same time
Two jackasses cannot bray at the same time
People must not speak all at once; it is important to listen
to each other.

402. Walk betta dan siddong
It is better to walk than to sit
Every effort has its reward;
It is always better to try.

403. Walk bout peteta nebber bear
A potato that has no abiding place will not grow
Find some stability in your life or it will be impossible to prosper.

404. Wall hab aise
Wall has ears
Be aware of your surroundings,
you don't know who may be listening.

405. Want all lose all
If you want all you'll lose all
Those who want everything for themselves may end up getting
nothing.

406. Wanti wanti caan get ih, getti getti noh want ih
*Those who want it cannot get it, those who get/
have it don't want it*
Those who want something badly often cannot get it
while those who have it don't appreciate it.

407. Wah ah fi yu cyaan be unfiyu
What is for you, cannot then be not yours
You will eventually receive whatever is due to you,

Part I: Proverbs and Sayings

irrespective of the time it takes.

408. Wah ah fun fi bwoy ah det fi bullfrag
What is fun to a boy is death to a frog
What one person finds funny the other person finds painful.

409. Wah noh cost nutten gib good meja
What costs nothing gives good measure
People tend to be generous with items that are of no cost to them.

410. Wah drop offa head drop pon shoulder
What drops from the head falls onto the shoulder
He who makes the effort often does not reap the rewards; Sometimes an item that was meant for you is given instead to members of your family.

411. Wah good fi di goose good fi di gander
What is good for the goose is good for the gander
Treat people fairly!

412. Wah noh happn inna year happen inna day
What doesn't happen in a year happens in a day
A long awaited event can happen suddenly;
There isn't always a precursor to an occurrence.
(Similar to: It's never too late for a shower of rain)

413. Wah noh kill fatten
What doesn't kill fattens
If an experience doesn't destroy you, it makes you stronger

414. Wah sweet nanny goat ah go run im belly
What is sweet to a nanny goat now will later give him diarrhoea
The things that seem enjoyable to you in one moment can hurt you later.

415. Wah sweet yuh gwine sour yuh
What is sweet to you will become sour
The source of your enjoyment now could cause you pain later.

416. Wat dawg si im bark all night, ram goat si ih noh trouble im
What a dog sees makes it bark all night; a ram goat sees it but it doesn't trouble him

People are affected and behave differently in situations.

417. Wat yuh doan know olda dan yuh
What you don't know is older than you
Knowledge comes with age and experience.

418. Wah gone bad ah morning, cyaan come good ah evenin
What's gone bad in the morning cannot be good in the evening If a situation starts badly, it will end badly.

419. Weh dawgs are not invited bones are not provided
Where dogs are not invited bones are not provided
Don't go where you are not welcome.

420. Wen a lian sleep doan wake im
When a lion is asleep, don't wake him
When a bad situation has been put to rest, don't revisit it unnecessarily.

421. Wen ashes cole dawg sleep in dey
When ashes are cold a dog will sleep in it
When people lose their power, others take liberties/advantage.

422. Wen belly full man bruk pot
When a man's belly is full he breaks the pot
Once people get what they want their interest wanes.

423. Wen bull foot bruk im nyam wid monkey
When a bull's foot is broken he eats with monkeys
When the mighty falls he makes friends with the humble.

424. When bull get ole yuh tek plantain trash fi tie him
When a bull gets old you can use plantain trash to tie him
People who were once powerful are subject to ridicule when they lose their power.

425. When bull ole im feed ah fence side
When a bull is old it feeds at the side of the fence
Caution increases with age.

Part I: Proverbs and Sayings

Holy Trinity Cathedral, Kingston (above)
100 year old Shaare Shalom Synagogue, Kingston - one of four remaining sand floor synagogues in the world (below)

Jamaican Proverbs and Places and Symbols

Devon House, Kingston (above)
Cathedral St. Jago De La Vega, Spanish Town (below)

Part I: Proverbs and Sayings

Jamaica Conference Centre, Kingston (above)
The Blue Mountain Range (below)

Jamaican Proverbs and Places and Symbols

White Witch Golf Course, Montego Bay (above)
Sandcastles Harbour, St. Ann (below)

426. Wen chicken tie up cackroach waan explanation
When a chicken is tied up the cockroach wants an explanation
When your enemies appear too feeble, friendly or harmless, that's cause for suspicion; be careful.

427. Wen cackroach get inna trubble im well glad fi run go hide ah fowl-house
When a cockroach gets into trouble it is happy to hide in a hen house
People implement any available solution when they find themselves
in trouble. (Similar to: Any port in a storm)

428. Wen coco ripe ih muss buss
When a cocoa is ripe it must burst out of its pod
Whatever is on your mind will be revealed in due course.

429. Wen cackroach av party im noh ax fowl
When a cockroach throws a party he doesn't invite fowls
It's unwise to invite your enemies to dine with you.

430. Wen cotton tree come down nanny goat jump over ih
When a cotton tree falls, a nanny goat jumps over it
When the mighty falls the weak triumphs.

431. When cow cyaan get wahta fi wash him face im tek him tongue
When a cow can't get water it washes its face with its tongue
If you lack resources, make the best use of what you have; be creative!

432. Wen crab walk to much im luze im claw
When a crab walks too much it loses its claw
If you overuse an item it will eventually be rendered useless.

433. Wen dawg av money im buy cheese
When a dog has money it buys cheese
Fools squander their money on things they
don't even like.

434. Wen dawg lib well im trubble cow, cow kick im
When a dog has a good life he interferes with cows and

they kick him
People who have nothing to do will interfere with others and eventually get hurt.

435. Wen dressa fall dung mawga dawg laugh
When a dresser falls down a meagre dog laughs
One man's loss is another man's gain.

436. Wen fiah an water mek fren anybody can lib
When fire and water become friends people can live
When mortal enemies bury the hatchet peace will reign.

437. Wen fish come outta sea an tell yuh alligator have fever, believe im
When a fish comes out of the sea and tells you that the alligator has fever, believe it!
Listen and learn from those who have experience.

438. Wen herring mawga im bone show
When a herring is meagre, its bones will protrude
Evil deeds will eventually be exposed.

439. Wen Jackass back strong dem overload im hamper
When a donkey is strong its owner tends to overload its hamper
Good workers are usually given more than their fair share of work to do.

440. Wen Jackass smell caarn im gellop
When a horse smells corn it gallops
If you treat people well they will work hard.
(Similar to: "Encouragement sweetens labour)

441. Wen jankro fly too high im fedda fall
When a crow flies too high it loses its feathers
If you act like you are better than everyone else you will eventually be humbled.

442. Wen one door shut annoda one open
When one door closes another one opens
There will always be opportunities for the taking; it is up to you to find them.

443. Wen pot full ih ovaflow

Part I: Proverbs and Sayings

When a pot is full it overflows
If you continuously provoke people one day they will retaliate.

444. Wen rat like fi romp roun puss jaw one day im gwine en up inna puss craw
When a rat likes to romp around a cat's jaw,
one day it will end up in the cat's craw
If you flirt with danger, you will eventually get hurt.

445. Wen snake bite yuh, yuh si lizzard yuh run
When you have been bitten by a snake you run from a lizard
Painful experiences cause people to become overly cautious.

446. Wen trubble tek yuh pickney shut fit yuh
When trouble takes you a child's shirt will fit you
When you are in trouble, you accept any help available.
(Similar to: A drowning man holds on to a straw)

447. Wen two dawg fight over bone annoda dawg run weh wid ih
When two dogs are fighting over a single bone;
another dog comes and takes it away
Ardent contenders often lose the prize to someone else.

448. When tail cut off God Almighty brush fly
When the tail gets cut off, God Almighty brushes off the flies
God helps those who are unable to help themselves.

449. Wen visita come ah wi fireside wi mek wi pot smell nice
When visitors come to our fireside, we ensure that our pot smells nice
Be hospitable to your guests and exhibit good manners in their presence.

450. Wen water trow weh ih cyaan pick up
When water spills, it cannot be picked up
It's no use complaining or pining over something that has already done. (Don't cry over spilt milk!)

451. Wen yellow snake ded yuh can meja im
When a (poisonous) yellow snake dies, you can measure him
The dead has no power over the living.

452. Wen yuh cyaan fight bushman yuh tek weh im bush
If you are unable to fight a bushman just take away his bush
If you are unable to overcome your enemy remove his protection or power source.

453. Wen yuh cyaan get dawg fi bark yuh mus tek sheep
When you cannot get a dog to bark, try using a sheep
If you don't have the ideal resources for what you want to do, try using something else; be creative!

454. Wen yuh fan fly yuh hat up sore
When you fan flies, you irritate the sore
Attempting to do damage control can make a bad situation worse.

455. Wen yuh get fambily bikkle nyam ih; when yuh hea fambily row, run!
When your family offers you food, accept it but when you hear family disputes, run!
Eat and drink with your family but do all you can to avoid getting involved in family disputes.

456. Wen yuh go ah fireside an si food eat half an lef half
When you go to a fireside and see some food, eat half of it and leave the other half
Don't disclose everything you know; keep some information to yourself.

457. Wen yuh go ah Jackass yaad yuh noh fi chat bout big aise
When you go to a Jackass' yard, do not talk about big ears
Avoid saying anything that could be construed as a criticism or insult to someone while you are on their property.

458. Wen yuh han inna lian mouth tek time draw ih out
When your hand is in a lion's mouth, carefully remove it
When you are in a vulnerable position you must be humble.

459. Wen yuh neighbour beard ketch ah fiah tek wahta wet fi yuh
If you see your neighbour's beard on fire, use water to wet yours

Learn from other people's experiences; don't wait until it happens to you!

460. Wen yuh see others ah jump pon two leg yuh jump pon one
When you see others jumping on two legs, you need to jump on one only
Don't follow the crowd; there is nothing wrong with being different.

461. Weh yuh boun yuh mus obey
Where you are bound you must obey
Honour your commitments and fulfil your responsibilities.

462. Wah fit masquita cyaan fit elephant
What fits a mosquito cannot fit an elephant
Not every style or situation will suit everyone.
(Similar to: Different strokes for different folks)

463. Who di cap fit mek dem wear it
Whoever the cap fits should be allowed to wear it
A guilty conscience will always feel targetted.

464. Who God bless no man curse
He who God blesses, no man can curse
If God has blessed you, no one can hurt you.

465. Wilful waste woeful want
Wilful waste woeful want
If you waste resources, you will live to regret it.

466. Wise sayla cyaa more ballast dan sail
A wise sailor carries more ballast than sails
Mere words without deeds are meaningless.
(Similar to: Actions speak louder than words)

467. Words inna mout ah noh load pan head
Words of the mouth are not loads on the head
Don't allow people's words to hurt you, ignore them!

468. Yeye fi si an aise fi hear but mout mus shut
The eyes should see and ears should hear but the mouth must remain closed

Listen and observe but don't participate in gossip.

469. Yuh cyaan wase shot pan blackbud - ih cyaan eat
Don't waste your resources trying to kill blackbirds – they are not edible
Don't waste your resources on people or items that will be of no use to you.

470. Yuh fraid fi yeye yuh nebber nyam head
If you are afraid of the eye, you will never eat the head
If you take people's negative comments too seriously you will never succeed.

471. Yuh get yuh han inna deble mout tek time tek ih out
If you put your hand in the devils mouth, take it out carefully
Exercise caution when you find yourself in tricky situations.

472. Yuh nebber see kickin cow widout kickin calf
You will never a see kicking cow without a kicking calf
Children imitate their parents.

473. Yuh nebber si pop-gun kill alligetta
One cannot use a pop-gun to kill an alligator
Don't send a boy to do a man's job.

474. Yuh nebber si smoke widout fiah
Where there's smoke there's fire
Suspicions and rumours are often based on facts.

475. Young bud noh know bout storm
A young bird doesn't know about storms
Young people lack life experience and are prone to making decisions that may be to their detriment.

476. Young bud noh know haard time
A young bird doesn't know hard times
Young people don't understand the challenges of life.

477. Young bud noh know wen berry ripe ah mounten
A young bird doesn't know when there are ripe berries in the mountain
There is much to learn from the experience and knowledge of older people.

478. Yuh bes fren ah yuh woss enemy
Your best friend is your worst enemy
Those who are closest to you are in a position to hurt you the most.

479. Yuh can hide an buy lan but yuh cyaan hide an wuk ih
You can hide and buy land but you can't hide and work on it
What is in the dark will ultimately be revealed.

480. Yuh can tek de hawse to the wahta but yuh cyaan mek im drink ih
You can take the horse to the water but you can't make it drink
You cannot make an individual do something that they really don't want to do.

481. Yuh come yah fi drink milk yuh noh come yah fi count cow!
You came here to drink milk, not to count cows
Accept people's kindness and don't meddle in their business; Don't worry about details that don't concern you.

482. Yuh cyaan expect anyting from a hog but a grunt
You can't expect anything from a pig but a grunt
People are true to their character, even if they try to hide it.

483. Yuh cyaan mek a silk purse outta pig aise
You cannot use a pig's ear to make a silk purse
You cannot change people.

484. Yuh cyaan mek blood outta stoane
It is not possible to get blood out of a stone
When resources are limited you have to make the best use of what is available.

485. Yuh cyaan plant peas an reap corn
You can't plant peas and expect to reap corn
You will reap exactly what you sow.

486. Yuh cyaan siddong pon bucket an draw water
You cannot sit on the bucket and draw water
Success is achieved not merely by having the appropriate resources, but by making good use of them.

487. Yuh cyaan siddong pon cow back an cuss cow kin
You cannot sit on a cow's back and curse the cow's skin
If you are dependent on someone you should not be Disrespectful to them.

488. Yuh cyaan tap bud from fly ova yuh head but yuh can
tap im fram mek nes in deh
You cannot prevent a bird from flying over your head but you can stop him from making a nest in it
You will meet and have dealings with people of questionable character but it is you who ultimately determines who becomes your friend.

489. Yuh cyaan tan blow no play wid tick
If you can't take blows, don't play with sticks
Don't venture into areas where you cannot handle all the possible consequences.

490. Yuh cyaan tek medicine fi smaddy else
You cannot take medicine for someone else
Everyone must expect to shoulder his own responsibility.

491. Yuh cyaan cut off yuh nose fi spite yuh feace
You must not cut off your nose in order to spite your face
Don't take actions that will ultimately hurt you just to get even with someone.

492. Yuh fallaw fool yuh fool yuself
If you follow a fool, you become a fool yourself
Be mindful of the company you keep.

493. Yuh gi dawg food inna plate im tek ih out put pan grung
When you feed a dog in a plate it takes out the food and places it on the ground
Some people aren't accustomed to quality so there is no point forcing it onto them.

494. Yuh know weh yuh barn but yuh noh know weh you ah go bury

Part I: Proverbs and Sayings

Puerto Seco Beach, St. Ann (above)
Doctor's Cave Beach, Montego Bay (below)

Jamaican Proverbs and Places and Symbols

Seven Mile Beach, Negril (above)
Frenchman's Cove, Port Antonio (below)

Part I: Proverbs and Sayings

Hellshire Beach – St. Catherine (above)
Winnifred Beach - Portland (below)

Jamaican Proverbs and Places and Symbols

Night in Half Way Tree (above)
Half Way Tree Transport Centre (below)
St Andrew

Part I: Proverbs and Sayings

*You know where you were born but you don't know
where you will be buried*
The past is known, the future is uncertain.

495. Yuh lick di spoon an lose di spoonful
You lick the spoon and lose the spoonful
Don't focus on micro gains when significant spoils are available for the taking.
(Similar to: Penny wise, pound foolish)

496. Yuh life lang but yuh cayliss wid ih
Your life is long but you are careless with it
Careless people take unnecessary risks.

497. Yuh mek yuh sail too big fi yuh boat yuh sail wi capsize yuh
If you make your sail too big for your boat your sail will cause your boat to capsize
Do not commit to performing a task that is clearly beyond your capability.

498. Yuh mus creep befoe yuh walk
You must creep before you walk
Take things progressively in stages.
(Similar to: Rome wasn't built in a day)

499. Yuh nebber know de use ah yuh battam till boil bruk out
You never know the use of your bottom until a boil breaks out
You don't appreciate the usefulness of something
until you no longer have it.

500. Yuh noh done breed so noh laugh afta yuh granny
*If you are still of childbearing age, don't laugh at
your grandmother*
Be respectful to the elderly; one day you too will be old.

501. Yuh pickney ah go bite yuh aise
Your child is going to bite your ears
If you don't discipline your child you will live to regret it.

502. Yuh promise sensé fowl anyting im ah look fi ih
If you make a promise to a chicken, he expects you to keep it

Don't make promises you cannot keep.

503. Yuh pushi, pushi, pushi till yuh shub ih
You push it, push it and push it until you shove it
If you consistently pester someone they will eventually retaliate.

504. Yuh right han haffi know wah yuh lef han ah du
Your right hand has to know what your left hand is doing
Learn to work in harmony with others for optimum results.

505. Yuh shake man han yuh noh shake im heart
You can shake a man's hand but not his heart
You can never know for sure what someone is thinking; superficial expressions are not necessarily reflections
of the heart.

506. Yuh si hous tan up, yuh noh go inside, yuh noh know ow ih tan
You don't know the true state of a house until you enter
Until you get to the bottom of a story it is unwise to
draw a conclusion.

Part I: Proverbs and Sayings

1. Afta tree nuh grow inna mi face
After all I don't have a tree growing in my face
I am not that unattractive that I can't find myself a partner.

2. Ca-ca faat!
What a surprise
That's incredible!

3. Carry-go bring-come
Carry go, bring come
Gossip

4. Country come ah town
Country has come to town
Someone who is not accustomed to city life is now experiencing it.

5. Di place chakka chakka
The place is untidy
The place needs sorting out; the place is in a state of chaos.

6. Doah use im fat fi fry me
Do not use his fat to fry me
Do not judge me because of another person's behaviour.

7. Enough fi stone dawg
Enough to stone a dog
An abundance of something.

8. Feel like Gumbeh drum widout goat kin
Feel like a Gumbeh drum without a goat skin
Feel out of place.

9. Fi me an yuh yeye mek four
Our eyes made four
We made direct eye contact.

10. From mi yeye deh a mi knee
From my eyes were at my knees
From I was very young

11. Fram saltfish a shingle house
From the days when salt fish was being used to shingle houses
Activities that took place a long time ago.

12. Fram Whappy kill Phillup
From the time that Whappy killed Phillup
A long time ago; way back when.

13. Gi laugh fi peas soup
Give laughs for peas soup
Make jokes and enjoy yourself

14. Gi im sponge fi go dry up sea
Give him a sponge to dry up the sea
Give someone an impossible task to perform.

15. Gi yuh a inch yuh tek a mile
I give you an inch and you take a mile
You always want more.

16. Gi yuh basket fi carry water
Give you a basket to carry water
Someone gave you a raw deal.

17. Heng pan nail
Hung on a nail
Tired-looking; disheveled

18. Hell an powdahouse
Hell and powderhouse
Extreme hullabaloo

19. Horse dead, cow fat
The horse is dead, the cow is fat
(The person) is talking nonsense.

20. Lawd tek de case an gi me de pillow
Lord, please take the case and give me the pillow
Lord, help me!

21. Long run short ketch
Catch you in the long run
It's only a matter of time before you are caught.

22. Man duppy laugh 'haha', ooman duppy laugh 'kikikeeki / kekekenken
Male ghosts laugh one way, female ghosts laugh another way

Men and women are inherently different.

23. Me an yuh noh plaan gungo ah line
You and I don't plant gungo in adjoining plots.
We don't get on; we are neither friends nor companions.

24. Mi deh ya de look pan yuh, di better one
I am here looking at you, the better one.
I am not as prosperous as you.

25. Me noh barn big
I wasn't born big (as an adult)
I am not a fool; I have life experience.

26. Me noh hab blue boot fi go clime eleben step
I don't have a blue boots to climb eleven steps
I try to avoid situations that could end up in court.

27. Me ole but mi noh cowl
I am old but not cold
I may be old but I can still be of use (I am not dead yet).

28. Mi shame tree dead
My shame tree is dead
I'm not easily embarrassed.

29. Neva si, come si
Never see, come see
Someone who is not accustomed to having nice things suddenly acquires them and makes a public show of it.

30. Poppy show da wol
Poppy shows are in the world
Idiots abound!

31. Puss bruk cocanat inna yuh yeye
Pus broke coconut in your eye
You are quite presumptuous.

32. Room full all full yuh cyaan get a spoonfull
The room is full, you can't get a spoonful
The place is fully occupied.

33. Six ah one, alf a dozen ah de oder
On the one hand there's six and on the other there's half a dozen
Two situations may look different but are essentially the same.

34. So me buy ih, so me sell ih
Just like I bought it, so I sell it
I am telling you the story, exactly as it has been told to me.

35. Soppm inna soppm
Something is in something
There is more to this situation than meets the eye.

36. Suck salt thru wooden spoon
Suck salt through wooden spoon
There is extreme poverty.

37. Tan teddy
Stay steady
Keep steady/calm!

38. Tap yuh naize mek me aise nyam grass
Stop your noise and let my ears eat grass
Be quiet!

39. Tek bad tings mek laugh
Take bad things and laugh at them
The ability to laugh at a bad situation.

40. Water more dan flour
There is more water than flour
Resources are scarce; there is not enough to go round.

41. Yuh barn wen yuh mumma gone ah market
You were born when your mother had gone to the market
You are such a fool.

42. Yuh cawna dark
Your corner is dark
Your prospects aren't looking bright at the moment.

43. Yuh come wid yuh two long han
You came with your two long hands
To arrive empty-handed (not bearing gifts).

44. Yuh freepapa bun
Your free-paper has been burnt
Your free time is over; back to normal activities.

45. Yuh gwine pay fi roas an bwoile
You will pay for roast and boil
You will be punished severely.

46. Yuh jus big an swo-so so
You are just big good for nothing
Big-bodied and lazy.

47. Yuh mean like starapple
You are as mean as a star-apple
You are a very miserly person.

48. Yuh mussi barn backa cow
You must have been born behind a cow
You are absolutely backward and ignorant.

49. Yuh pick, pick, pick till u pick fart
You keep picking until you pick a fart
You examined several options and eventually chose the least attractive.

50. Yuh too red eye
Your eyes are too red
You are just too envious.

51. Yuh wi fine out weh water walk go a pungkin belly
You will find out how water gets into a pumpkin's core
You will discover, in one way or another (often used as a threat).

Part II

FOLK SONGS

Part II: Folk Songs

1. Banana

Wah oh, banana
Wah oh, banana
Green one, banana
Ripe one, banana

Come we go dung (x2)
Come we go dung ah Solas market
Come we go dung (2)
Fi go buy banana.

Tek out yuh lang lang treadbag
Fi go buy banana (x2)

Come we go dung (x2)
Come we go dung ah Solas market
Come we go dung, fi go buy banana
(Repeat)

Banana
Green one, banana
Ripe one, banana
Lacatan, banana
Gros Michel, banana
Chinese, banana
Robusta, banana
All kind, banana

Come we go dung...

2. Brown Girl in the Ring

Dere's a brown girl in di ring, tra la la la la
A brown girl in di ring tra la la la la
Dere's a brown girl in di ring tra la la la la
Shi luk lakka sugar an' a plum
(Plum Plum)

Show mi yuh motion tra la la la la
Show mi yuh motion tra la la la la

Show mi yuh motion tra la la la la
Show mi yuh motion tra la la la la la
Shi luk lakka sugar an' a plum
(Plum Plum)

Skip across the ocean tra la la la la
Skip across the ocean tra la la la la la
Skip across the ocean tra la la la la
Skip across the ocean tra la la la la la
Shi luk lakka sugar an' a plum
(Plum Plum)

Stand before yuh lover tra la la la la
Stand before yuh lover tra la la la la la
Stand before yuh lover tra la la la la
Shi luk lakka sugar an' a plum
(Plum Plum)

Dere's a brown girl in di ring tra la la la la
A brown girl in the ring tra la la la la la
Dere's a brown girl in di ring sha la la la la
Shi luk lakka sugar an' a plum
(Plum Plum)

3. Chi chi Bud

A Chi chi bud oh!
Some a dem ah holla some a bawl

Chi chi bud oh
Some a conlan; some a dem...
Some a blue foot; some a dem...
Tin tin; some a dem...
Chickman chick; some a dem...
Pea dove; some a dem...
Cling cling; some a dem...
Gawling; some a dem...
Gimme-me bit; some a dem...
Hawk; some a dem...
Some a jankrooo,
Some a dem a holla, some a bawl!

Part II: Folk Songs

4. Day Oh

Chorus
Day, mi sey day! mi sey day! mi sey day oh!
Day deh light an' me wan' go home (x2)

Come, Missa tally man, tally me banana
Day deh light an' me wan' go home. (Chorus)

Six han', seven han', eight han bunch!
Day deh light an' me wan' go home (x2)
(Chorus)

We load bananas till di early light
Day deh light an' me wan' go home. Sleep all day and wok all night

Day deh light an' me wan' go home.
(Chorus)

Mi com ya fe wok, mi noh come yah fi igle
Day deh light an' me wan' go home
Mi com ya fi wok, mi noh come yah fi igle
Day deh light an' me wan' go home.
(Chorus)

5. Dinah

Dinah Oh!
All de call mi call, mi call Dinah,
Dinah hear mi but shi wont answa
Sake a di pain ah back mi cyaan limba
An' me have five mile fi go walk.
(Repeat)

6. Dip Dem Bedward

Chorus
Dip dem Bedward, dip dem
Dip dem in di healing stream
Dip dem sweet but not too deep

Dip dem fi cure bad feeling.

(Chorus)

Some come from di nort' with dem face full ah wart
Dip dem in di healing stream
Some come from di sout' with dem big yabba mout'
Dip dem in di healing stream.

(Chorus)

Some come from di eas' lakka real leggo beas'
Dip dem in di healing stream
Some come from di wes' think dem a de bes'
Dip dem in di healing stream.
(Chorus)

7. Evenin' Time (Louise Bennett)

Come Miss Clare
Tek di bankra off yuh head mi dear
Evening breeze ah blow
Come dis way Miss Flo.

Help down yah
Afta yuh no beas' ah burd'n mah
Ress yuhself at ease
Feel di evenin' breeze.

Evenin' time
Work is over now its evenin' time
Wih deh walk pon mountain
Deh walk pan mountain
Deh walk pan mountainside.

Meck we cook wih bickle pan dih way
Meck wih eat an sing
Dance an play ring ding
Pan dih mountain side.

Ketch up dih fire Ma'hta
Pass me dih gungo peas

Part II: Folk Songs

Rub up dih flour Sarah - Lawd!
Feel di evenin' breeze.

8. Hill an Gully Ride

(Chorus)
Hill an' gully ride oh! hill an' gully (x2)
An' yuh bend dung low dung, hill an' gully (x2)
An yuh betta mine yuh tumble dung, hill an' gully
If yuh tumble dung yuh bruk yuh neck, hill an' gully.

9. Jane and Louisa

Jane and Louisa will soon come home
Soon come home, soon come home
Jane and Louisa will soon come home
Into this beautiful garden.
My love will you 'low me to waltz with you,
waltz with you, waltz with you
My love will you 'low me to waltz with you, into this
beautiful garden.

My love will you 'low me to pick a rose, pick a rose, pick a rose
My love will you 'low me to pick a rose,
Into this beautiful garden.

10. Linstead Market

(Chorus)
Carry mi ackee go a Linstead Market
Not a quattie worth sell
Carry me ackee go a Linstead Market
Not a quattie worth sell.
Lawd what a night not a bite
What a Satiday night
(x2)

Everybody come feel up, feel up
Not a quattie worth sell

Everybody come feel up, feel up
Not a quattie worth sell
(Chorus)

Do mi mammy nuh beat mi kill mi
Sake a merry-go-roun'
Do mi mammy don't beat me kill
Sake a merry-go-roun'

(Chorus)

All di pickney dem ah linga linga
Fi weh dem mumma noh bring
All di pickney dem ah linga linga
Fi weh dem mumma noh bring

(Chorus)

11. Liza - Waata Come a mi Yeye

Every time mi memba Liza
Waata come ah mi yeye
Wen mi tink pan mi nice gal Liza
Waata come ah mi yeye.

Come back Liza, come back gal
Wipe di cry fram mi yeye
Come back Liza, come back gal
Wipe di cry fram mi yeye.

12. Lizzy Jane

If yuh falaw dat ole man yuh neva married (x2)
Mr Joe, hole de train an lef Lizzy Jane
So she hallaw, so she puff so she bawl Oh!

13. Long Time Gal

Dis long time gal me never see yuh
Come mek me hold yuh hand

Part II: Folk Songs

Dis long time gal me never see yuh
Come mek me hold yuh hand.

Peel head John Crow sit up inna tree top a pick out the blossom
Mek mi hold yuh han, Gal
Mek mi hold yuh han'

Long time gal mi never see yuh
Come mek we walk and talk
Long time gal me never see yuh
Come mek we walk and talk.

Peel head John Crow sit upon di tree top a pick out the blossom
Mek mi walk an' talk Gal
Mek mi walk an' talk.

Long time gal mi never see yuh
Come mek we wheel an' tun
Long time gal mi never see yuh
Come mek we wheel an' tun.

Peel head John Crow sit up inna tree top a pick out di blossom
Mek we wheel an' tun Gal
Mek we wheel an' tun

14. Manuel Road

Guh dung a Manuel Road gal an' bwoy
Fi go bruk rackstone (gal an' bwoy) (x2)

Bruk dem one by one (gal an' bwoy)
Bruk dem two by two (gal an' bwoy)
Bruk dem one by three (gal an' bwoy)
Bruk dem two by four (gal an' bwoy)
Bruk dem one by five (gal an' bwoy)

Finger mash noh cry (gal an' bwoy)
Memba ah play we ah play (gal an' bwoy)

Guh dung a Manuel Road gal an' bwoy
Fi go bruk rackstone (gal an' bwoy)

Bruk dem one by one (gal an' bwoy)...

15. Mango Time

Mi nuh drink coffee tea mango time
Care how nice it may be mango time
In the heat of the mango crop
When di fruit dem a ripe an drop
Wash your pot turn dem down mango time

Di terpentine large an fine, mango time
Robin mango so sweet, mango time
Number eleven an' hairy skin
Pack di bankra an' ram dem in
For di bankra mus' full, mango time
Mek wi go ah mango walk, mango time
For is only di talk mango time
Mek wi jump pon di big jackass
Ride im dung an no tap ah pass
Mek di best ah di crop, mango time.

16. Moonshine Tonight

Moon shine tonight come mek we dance an' sing
Moon shine tonight come mek we dance an' sing

Chorus
Mi deh rock so, you deh rock so
Unda banyan tree
Mi deh rock so, you deh rock so
Unda banyan tree

Ladies may curtz and gentlemen may bow
Ladies may curtz and gentlemen may bow
(Chorus)

Come we join hands and mek we dance an' sing
Come we join hands and mek we dance an' sing
(Chorus)

Part II: Folk Songs

17. Nobody's Business

Chorus
Nobody's business, business
Nobody's business, business
Nobody's business but me own
Nobody's business, business
Nobody's business, business
Nobody's business but me own

Solomon Grundy gone ah Ecuador
Lef' im wife an' pickney out-a-door
Nobody's business but me own
Solomon Grundy gone ah Ecuador
Lef' im wife an' pickney out-a-door
Nobody's business but me own.
(Chorus)

If ah married to a naygaman
An ah lef' 'im for a chinaman
Nobody's business but me own
If ah married to a naygaman
An ah lef' 'im for a chinaman
Nobody's business but me own.
(Chorus)

18. Sammy Dead Oh!

Sammy plant piece a carn dung ah gully, hm mm
an ih bear till ih kill poah Sammy, hm.mm

Sammy dead, Sammy dead, Sammy dead oh! Hm mm
Sammy dead, Sammy dead, Sammy dead oh! Hm, mm.

Ah nuh tief Sammy tief mek dem kill im, hm mm (x2)
But a grudgeful, yes a grudgeful mek dem kill im, hm mm (x2)

Neighbour cyan bear fi si neighbour flourish, hm mm (x2)
Sammy dead, Sammy dead, Sammy dead oh! Hm mm (x2)

19. Shine Yeye Gyal

A shine yeye gyal is a trubble to a man (x3)
Shi want an' shi waan an' shi want everyting

Har lip fava libba an' shi waan lipstick (x3)
Shi want an' she waan an' she want everyting

Har waist fava wire an' shi waan broad belt (x3)
Shi waan an shi want an shi want everyting.
(Repeat 1st verse)

20. Under the Coconut Tree

It was under di coconut tree, darling
It was under di coconut tree
You promised to marry to me darling
It was under di coconut tree.

Let's go under di coconut tree, darling
Let's go under di coconut tree
'twas dere dat you promised your love, darling
Let's go under di coconut tree.

Part III

SYMBOLS, PEOPLE, PLACES & THINGS

Part III: Symbols, People, Places and Things

Jamaica – Land of Wood and Water

Jamaica is a beautiful place and Jamaicans are an amazing people. We are well known for our beaches, delicious food and Reggae music, but as a people we have progressed way beyond the obvious and have excelled and impacted in almost every sphere of life. Here we present a taste of Jamaica – a few of the people who have made contributions, national symbols, customs, fauna and flora.

Communication – Jamaica has a fully digital telephone communication system (landline, internet, mobile and entertainment)

Culture – Jamaica is rich in culture and has a strong global presence. The musical genres reggae, ska, mento, rocksteady, dub, and, more recently, dancehall and ragga all originated on the island.

Currency – Jamaica's currency is the Jamaican dollar. Bank notes are issued for the following amounts: J$50, J$100, J$500, J$1000 and J$5000.

Economy – Jamaica is a mixed economy with both state enterprises and private sector businesses. Major sectors of the Jamaican economy include agriculture, mining, manufacturing, tourism, and financial and insurance services.

Geography – Jamaica is the third largest Caribbean island, measuring 145 miles (234 km) at its widest point. The climate in Jamaica is tropical, with hot and humid weather, although higher inland regions are more temperate. There is no definite rainy season but it rains mostly in May and October.

Government and Politics – Jamaica is an independent state with an elected Parliament, a Prime Minister, an elected House of Representatives and a Senate. The head of state is Queen Elizabeth II and her representative on the island is the Governor General. Jamaica is a member of the Commonwealth of Nations.

Education – Education is free from the early childhood to secondary levels.

History – Arawak and Taino indigenous people originating from South America settled on the island between 4000 and 1000 BC. Columbus arrived in 1494 and claimed Jamaica for Spain. The Spanish were defeated by the British in 1655 and the country achieved independence from Britain on 6 August 1962.

Industries – tourism, bauxite, agriculture (sugar, bananas, coffee, pimento, cocoa and tobacco).

Language – The official language of Jamaica is English. Jamaicans also speak Jamaican Patois, which has become known widely through the spread of Reggae music.

Population – Just under 3,000,000 people from the following ethnic groups: African, Indian, Chinese, Lebanese, Syrian, English, Scottish, Irish, and German.

Religion – Christians make up the majority of the population. Other popular religions in Jamaica include Islam, Baháʼí Faith, Buddhism, and Hinduism and Jews.

Sports – Cricket, athletics and football are popular; other sports include boxing, horseracing, golf, netball, volleyball, chess, basketball and dominoes.

Transport – Road, rail, sea and air transport, with roadways forming the backbone of the island's internal transport system.

Part III: Symbols, People, Places and Things

Map of Jamaica

Our Neighbours

National Symbols

National Flag

The Flag was first raised on Independence Day - 6 August 1962. It depicts memories of past achievements and provides inspiration for further success. Black represents the strength and creativity of the people which allows them to overcome the odds, yellow for the golden sunshine and green for the lush vegetation of the island.

Coat of Arms

The Jamaican national motto - Out of Many One People – is based on the population's multiracial roots. The Coat of Arms shows a male and a female member of the Taino tribe standing on either side of a shield which bears a red cross with five golden pineapples. The crest is a Jamaican crocodile mounted on the Royal Helmet of the British Monarchy and mantling.

National Flower Lignum Vitae (Guiacum officinale)

The Lignum Vitae (wood of life) has medicinal qualities. The plant is extremely ornamental, producing an attractive blue flower and orange-yellow fruit. The tree is one of the most useful in the world. The body, gum, bark, fruit, leaves and blossom all serve some useful purpose.

National Bird the Doctor Bird (Trochilus polytmus)

The doctor bird or swallow tail humming bird is found only in Jamaica. Its beautiful feathers have no counterpart in the entire bird population and they produce iridescent colours characteristic only of that family. The mature male has two long tails which stream behind him when he flies.

Part III: Symbols, People, Places and Things

National Tree – The Blue Mahoe (Hibiscus Elatus)

The Blue Mahoe is indigenous to the island and grows quite rapidly. It has a straight trunk, broad green leaves and hibiscus-like flowers which change colour from bright yellow to orange red and finally to crimson. The Blue Mahoe is used for timber, making furniture and for making decorative objects. Cuba is the only other place where the Blue Mahoe grows naturally.

National Fruit – The Ackee

(Blighia sapida)

Originally imported to the island from West Africa, Ackee is derived from the original name Ankye which comes from the Twi language of Ghana. There are two main types of ackees - soft yellow 'butter' ackee and hard, cream-coloured 'cheese' ackee. The fruit contains a poison (hypoglcin) which is dissipated when it is properly harvested and cooked.

National Dish Ackee & Saltfish

This is a tasty dish made with ackee, codfish, tomatoes, peppers onions, black pepper and pimento. Serve with fried or boiled dumplings, roast **breadfruit, hard dough bread**, or boiled green **bananas**.

Jamaica's National Heroes

Sir Alexander Bustamante (1884-1977)

A charismatic and impressive speaker and leader who understood the dynamics of labour relations. The years 1937 and 1938 brought the outbreak of widespread discontent and social unrest and Bustamante became the champion of the working class. In 1943 he founded the Jamaica Labour Party (JLP), and in 1962 became the first Prime Minister of Independent Jamaica.

Norman Washington Manley (1893-1969)

A brilliant scholar, athlete, soldier and lawyer, Manley identified with the cause of the workers at the time of the labour troubles of 1938 and in September of that year founded the People's National Party (PNP). He was elected PNP President annually until he retired in 1969. Manley's and Bustamante's efforts resulted in the New Constitution of 1944 granting full Adult Suffrage.

Marcus Mosiah Garvey (1887-1940)

Garvey sought the unification of all Blacks through the establishment of the United Negro Improvement Association (UNIA) which he started in 1914 and he spoke out against economic exploitation and cultural denigration. The UNIA, which grew into an international organisation, encouraged self-government for

Paul Bogle (1822-1865)

A baptist deacon is generally regarded as a peaceful man but poverty and injustice in the society and lack of public confidence in the central authority urged Bogle to lead a protest march to the Morant Bay courthouse on 11 October 1865. He was captured and hanged on October 24, 1865 but his actions paved the way for the establishment of just practices in the courts and led to a change in official attitude

black people worldwide; self-help economic projects and protest against racial discrimination.

George William Gordon (1820-1865)

A self-educated landowner in St. Thomas who urged people to protest against and resist the oppressive and unjust conditions under which they were forced to live. He was arrested and charged, illegally tried by Court Martial, convicted, and executed on 23 October 1865. His death, along with that of Paul Bogle triggered the beginning of a new era in Jamaica's development - the British government became compelled to effect changes including outstanding reforms in education, health, local government, banking and infrastructure.

which in turn enhanced the social and economic conditions of people.

Samuel Sharpe (1801-1832)

"I would rather die upon yonder gallows than live in slavery". Because of his intelligence and leadership qualities, Sam Sharpe became a "daddy", or leader of the native Baptists in Montego Bay. An educated town slave, preacher and spokesman Sharpe carried on the Resistance against slavery and effected the most outstanding Slave Rebellion in Jamaica's history. The 1831 Rebellion started in St. James on December 28 and spread throughout the entire island. Sam Sharpe was eventually captured and hung at the Parade in Montego Bay (now Sam Sharpe Square). In 1834 the Abolition Bill was passed by the British Parliament and in 1838 slavery was abolished.

Nanny of the Maroons

A leader of the Maroons at the beginning of the 18th century, Nanny was regarded by both the Maroons and the British settlers as an outstanding military leader who became a symbol of unity and strength for her people during times of crisis. She possessed a fierce fighting spirit and her cleverness in planning guerrilla warfare confused the British who dreaded the Maroon traps set for them. Nanny met her untimely death sometime around 1734. Yet, the spirit of Nanny of the Maroons remains today as a symbol of that indomitable desire that will never yield to captivity.

Part III: Symbols, People, Places and Things

Out of Many, One People

Jamaican children
(Photo courtesy of the JTB)

Jamaica has a dynamic culture and a diverse population representing the mosaic of ethnic groups that landed on the island's shores over the past several centuries.

Whether they be descendants of the colonists or more recent immigrants from other countries, people of all nationalities live and work in harmony in Jamaica. Afro-Jamaicans constitute over 90% with the remaining percentage shared among English, Scottish, Welsh, East Indians, Chinese, Lebanese, Syrians, Jews and others. This diversity is the essence of the island's motto "Out of Many, One People".

National Anthem

The Anthem is the creative work of: The late Rev. & Hon. Hugh Sherlock, OJ, OBE; The late Hon. Robert Lightbourne, OJ; The late Mapletoft Poulle, and Mrs Poulle (now Mrs Raymond Lindo)

Eternal Father bless our land,
Guard us with Thy Mighty Hand
Keep us free from evil powers,
Be our light through countless hours.
To our Leaders Great Defender,
Grant true wisdom from above.
Justice, Truth be ours forever,
Jamaica Land we love.
Jamaica, Jamaica, Jamaica land we love.

Teach us true respect for all,
Stir response to duty's call.
Strengthen us the weak to cherish,
Give us vision lest we perish.
Knowledge send us Heavenly Father,
Grant true wisdom from above.
Justice, Truth be ours forever,
Jamaica, land we love.
Jamaica, Jamaica, Jamaica land we love.

Code for use of the National Anthem

Everyone should stand at attention, (i.e., heels together) at the playing of the National Anthem and men should remove their hats. The first verse should be played or sung as specifically designated on the arrival of the Governor-General or the Prime Minister. The National Anthem may be sung or played at public gatherings. Singing of the National Anthem should form part of the ceremony of raising and lowering of the flag at the beginning and end of term in schools and at Independence celebrations.

Part III: Symbols, People, Places and Things

National Song: I Pledge my Heart

I pledge my heart forever
To serve with humble pride
This shining homeland, ever
So long as earth abide.

I pledge my heart, this island
As God and faith shall live
My work, my strength, my love and
My loyalty to give.

O green isle of the Indies,
Jamaica, strong and free,
Our vows and loyal promises
O heartland, 'tis to Thee.

National Pledge

Before God and all mankind
I pledge the love and loyalty of my heart
The wisdom and courage of my mind
The strength and vigour of my body
In the service of my fellow citizens.

I promise to stand up for justice
Brotherhood and peace
To work diligently and creatively
To think generously and honestly
So that, Jamaica may, under God, increase in beauty
Fellowship and prosperity
And play her part in advancing the welfare of the whole human race.

Shorter Pledge for Schools

Before God and all mankind
I pledge my love, my loyalty and skills, in the service of Jamaica and my fellow citizens.

I promise to work diligently and to help build a prosperous and peaceful nation.

National Prayer

Let us give thanks for all God's goodness and the wonderful heritage into which we have entered:
Response to each petition: We give thee thanks, O God

For Jamaica, our island home, the land of our birth -
Response

For the majesty of our hills, the beauty of our valleys, and the flaming loveliness of our gardens –
Response

For the warmth and brightness of our days and the calm and peace of our countryside –
Response

For the rich heritage of our people coming for many races, and yet one in purpose, in achievement, and in destiny, and for the dignity of labour and the service given by every citizen of our land –
Response

For freedom, just laws and our democratic way of life –
Response

For the high privilege and responsibility of Independence and for bringing us to nationhood –
Response

For our parents, teachers, religious and other leaders and all those who in every walk of life are helping to prepare us for responsible citizenship, and for all those who are giving voluntary service in the public interest –
Response

For the poets, artists and thinkers and all who create in us the vision of a new and better society –
Response

For our godly heritage, the example of Jesus Christ and the sacrifices of our fathers in the faith –
Response

Ethnic Groups

The Africans
With the overwhelming majority of Jamaicans being of African descent, their contribution has been remarkable and many have excelled to secure Jamaica's place and reputation in the international arena. They are far too many to number but they include: George Steibel, the island's first black millionaire who built Devon House, Marcus Garvey, Black Nationalist and National Hero and more contemporarily, Bob Marley, worldwide musical superstar and the Hon. Louise Bennett-Coverley, cultural icon.

The Chinese
The Chinese community in Jamaica contributes tremendously to the country. It includes writers like Anglican priest Easton Lee, beauty queens such as Sheila Chung and Patsy Yuen, MPs such as Rose Leon, Ferdinand Yap-Sam and Delroy Chuck, business people controlling substantial restaurant, bakery and supermarket chains such as Island Grille, Purity and SuperPlus, as well as banks such as NCB.

The English
It is not difficult to see reminders of English colonisation in Jamaica. You only have to look at the structure of the government, judicial systems, civil service, military, police and education systems, religious institutions (protestant churches), place names and even some of our traditional food and drink. The development of sport (cricket and football) was greatly influenced by the English.

The Germans
There are several areas in Jamaica where Germans settled and where their descendants are still present today. These include areas of Seaford Town, Brown's Town, Alexandria, Christiana, Stewart Town and Ulster Spring. There are also places whose

names reflect German influence such as Manhertz Gap, Charlotten-burgh, Mount Holstein, Bremen Valley, New Brunswick and Hessen Castle.

The Indians
Descendants of the immigrant workers have influenced the fields of farming, medicine, politics and even horse-racing. Names such as Chatani, Chulani, Tewani, Mahtani, Daswani, Vaswani and Chandiram have become synonymous with manufacturing, wholesale, retail and in-bond businesses providing employment for thousands of Jamaicans.

The Irish
There are many prominent Jamaicans of Irish heritage. These include poet Claude McKay, Chris Blackwell, founder of Island Records, one of Jamaica's foremost historians and former UWI Vice Chancellor - Sir Philip Sherlock, writer John Hearne, and successful horse trainer, Phillip Feanny, Surnames such as Burke, Collins, Mackey, Murphy and Madden, to name just a few, are quite common.

The Japanese
Although the Japanese were not early settlers in Jamaica, Japanese people now live on the island and many Japanese nationals take a musical pilgrimage to Jamaica. In recent times, they have embraced Jamaica's reggae/dancehall culture. Not only are there reggae artistes from the Land of the Rising Sun but there are also sound systems such as the famous Mighty Crown, which won the coveted Death Before Dishonour title.

In 2002 'Junko Bashment' a young Japanese was crowned Dancehall Queen at the annual contest where talented women make strong fashion statements and display exceptional dance moves. Pushim, a singer dubbed 'Queen of Japanese Reggae', recorded her first album "Say Greeting" in Jamaica and has performed at Reggae Sumfest.

The Jews
Prominent Jewish Jamaicans who made an impact include Poet Daniel Lopez Laguna who converted biblical Psalms into poems; 19th century painter Isaac Mendes Belisario whose famed "Belisario" prints of Jamaican characters are cultural icons; Jacob and Joshua de Cordova who founded the "Gleaner" in 1833; Ward

Theatre architect Rudolph Henriques; Jorge Ricardo Isaacs, author of 'Maria', considered the "national novel" of Columbia; Sir Neville Noel Ashenheim who served as Jamaica's first ambassador to Washington; the Hon. Ernest Altamont da Costa and Councillor Senator Hon. Eli Matalon, who served as Mayors of Kingston.

The Lebanese
The Lebanese gave the island a beauty queen - former Miss Jamaica and Miss World, Lisa Hanna-Panton is part Lebanese. Names like Hanna, Mahfood, Issa, Joseph, Ammar, Azan, Shoucair, Karam, Younis, Khouri, Fadil, Feanny, Dabdoub, Matalon and Ziadie are giants of retail, tourism, horse racing, industry and manufacturing. The most famous Jamaican with Lebanese descent is the Most Hon. Edward Seaga, former Prime Minister.

The Scottish
Perhaps the most infamous Scottish immigrant is Lewis Hutchison, better known as the Mad Master of Edinburgh Castle who was accused of killing travellers for sport. He was tried, found guilty and condemned to death by hanging in Spanish Town Square. More positive forms of Scottish influence can be found in Jamaican dance the scotch reel in Kingston's Scots Kirk Church, as well as in Jamaica's language.

The Welsh
The Welsh has shown their presence on the island through their buildings and craftsmanship including many of the slate roofs that covered Jamaican 18th & 19th century sugar works. There are also Welsh place names such as Bangor Ridge, Cardiff Hall, Llandilo, Llandovery and Pencarne. Jamaican surnames of Welsh background include: Bryan, Davis, Davies, Jones, Meredith, Morgan, Owens, Rhys/Reece, Williams and Vaughan.

Governors-General of Jamaica

Sir Kenneth **William Blackburne** (6 Aug – 30 Nov 1962)

The Rt. Hon. Sir Edward Zacca (31 Mar –1 Aug 1991) *(acting)*

The Most Hon. Sir Clifford Clarence Campbell (1 Dec 1962 – 2 Mar 1973)

The Most Hon. Sir Howard Felix Hanlan Cooke (1 Aug 1991- 15 Feb 2006)

Sir Herbert George Holwell Duffus (2 Mar – 27 Jun 1973) *(acting)*

The Most Hon. Prof. Sir Kenneth O. Hall (15 Feb 2006 -26 Feb 2009)

The Most Hon. Sir Florizel **Augustus** Glasspole (27 Jun 1973 – 31 Mar 1991)

His Excellency the Most Hon. Sir Patrick Linton Allen (26 Feb 2009 –present)

Part III: Symbols, People, Places and Things

Jamaica's Prime Ministers

Sir Alexander Bustamante (JLP)
Apr 1962 - Feb 1967

Sir Donald Sangster (JLP)
Feb 1967 - Apr 1967

Hugh Shearer (JLP)
Apr 1967 - Mar 1972

Michael Manley (PNP)
Mar 1972 - Nov 1980 & Feb 1989 - Mar 1992

Edward Seaga (JLP)
Nov 1980 - Feb 1989

P. J. Patterson (PNP)
Mar 1992 - Mar 2006

Portia Simpson-Miller (PNP)
Mar 2006 - Sept 2007 & Jan 2012 – Feb 2016

Bruce Golding (JLP)
Sept 2007- Sept 2011

Andrew Holness (JLP)
Oct. 2011 – Jan. 2012 & Feb. 2016 to Present

Distinguished Pioneers

Dr. the Hon. Louise Bennett Coverley, OM, OJ, MBE

(7 Sep 1919 –26 Jul 2006)

Folklorist, poet, and Cultural Ambassador

Louise Bennett captured the spontaneity of the expression of the Jamaican people - their joys and sorrows, their poignant wit, religion and philosophy of life. She lectured extensively in the USA and the UK on Jamaican folklore and music and represented Jamaica all over the world. Her contribution to Jamaican cultural life earned her an M.B.E., the Norman Manley Award for Excellence (in the field of Arts), the Order of Jamaica (1974) the Institute of Jamaica's Musgrave Silver and Gold Medals for distinguished eminence in the field of Arts and Culture, and in 1983 the Honorary Degree of Dr. of Letters from the University of the West Indies. In 1998 she received the Honorary Degree of Dr. of Letters from York University, Toronto, Canada.

The Jamaican Government appointed her Cultural Ambassador at Large for Jamaica and in 2001 she was awarded the Order of Merit for her distinguished contribution to the development of the Arts and Culture.

The Hon. Robert Nesta Marley, OM

(6 Feb 1945–11 May 1981)

Singer-songwriter, Reggae icon & Musical Ambassador

Bob Marley achieved worldwide greatness and is regarded as one of the greatest musical legends of our time. Proclaimed and accepted worldwide as the 'King of Reggae', he charted his own course in the entertainment industry as a songwriter, singer and performer. He successfully transcended three Jamaican musical genres from the 1960's through to the early 1980's - Ska, Rock Steady and Reggae. His music is still relevant to millions of people across the globe.

Bob Marley's song, 'One Love', was voted the best song of the 20th century, his album 'Exodus' (1977), stayed on the UK's music chart for 56 consecutive weeks and was voted the greatest album of the century by Time Magazine. He received the BBC's Song of the Millennium for "One Love".

In 1981 Bob Marley was awarded the order of Merit for his outstanding contribution to Jamaican culture. He was inducted into the Rock & Roll Hall of Fame and he received a Grammy Lifetime Achievement Award.

Part III: Symbols, People, Places and Things

Bob Marley Museum, Kingston (above)
and his Mausoleum in St. Ann (below)

Outstanding and Distinguished Jamaicans

THE ARTS

– Fine Arts

Alvin Marriot – Master Carver and sculptor, created the Olympic statue which now adorns our National Stadium. Many of his carvings and statues are on public display and in administrative buildings in Jamaica and the UK. In 1967 he received the Jamaica Badge of Honour.

Barrington Watson, CD, OJ –. Barrington Watson was born in Lucea and one of Jamaica's most talented artist. In 1967 he won a prize at the first Spanish Biennale at Barcelona. Watson has exhibited throughout Jamaica and internationally. He is the subject of Lennie Little-White's 2015 documentary film They Call Me Barrington.

Carl Myrie Abrahams OD – Abrahams was seen by some as 'the father of Jamaican art'. The National Gallery of Jamaica said series of 20 paintings of The Passion of Christ that "the devout sentiment of a true believer marked Abrahams as Jamaica and the Caribbean's finest religious painter. Two of his religious works were featured on Jamaican stamps, marking the advent of the third millennium.

Cecil Baugh OJ – The 'Master Potter' pioneered the art of modern ceramics in Jamaica and became probably the most influential 20th-century ceramic artist in the Caribbean.

Cecil Harvey Cooper, CD – Celebrated artist, educator, and tenor. He was taught by artists such as Barrington Watson and Albert Huie and gravitated to a style of painting known as expressive realism. Cooper worked mainly in paint media, using gestural painting and drawing techniques, and his thematic preoccupation with the joys and anxieties of the human condition.

Edna Manley OM – Sculptor who played a major pioneering role in the history of 20th century Jamaican art. Her works are in private collections, galleries and public buildings worldwide.

Gene Pearson, OD – He was a renowned sculptor and ceramic artist. His works are mostly inspired by the arts of ancient Nubia, Benin and the Rastafarian culture and in 2015 and was awarded the Silver Musgrave Medal from the Institute of Jamaica.

Gloria Escoffery, OD - She was a Jamaican painter, poet and art critic active in the 1940s and 1950. She received the Silver Musgrave from the Institute of Jamaica in 1985 and was inducted in the Caribbean Hall of Fame last year in 2001. Ms. Escoffery is one of 21 artists featured in the book A Celebration of Jamaican Art, published by the Jamaican Artists and Craftsmen Guild.

Keith Anthony Morrison CD – Painter, educator, critic, curator and administrator, he has exhibited his work internationally, including exhibitions at the Museums of Contemporary Art, Monterrey Mexico, Art Institute of Chicago, the Smithsonian Institution, the Cincinnati Museum, the Corcoran Gallery of Art; and the High Museum.

Mallica 'Kapo' Reynolds OD – Painter whose works have been exhibited widely both at home and abroad. They also form a part of the permanent collection of the National Gallery.

THE ARTS
– *Literature*

Anthony Winkler – One of Jamaica's most gifted and successful writers. In 1991 he wrote the screenplay for the film version of The Lunatic, and in 1999 his original screenplay - The Annihilation of Fish was made into a movie.

Barry Reckord - Pioneering Playwright whose work captured the conflicts of class and race in 1960s Britain. His award-winning play Skyvers, which was first produced at the Royal Court in London in 1963, was broadcast in a new BBC Radio 3 production. Reckord wrote two television dramas for the BBC, In the Beautiful Caribbean (1972) and Club Havana (1975).

Carolyn Cooper CD – Author and professor of literary and cultural studies at the University of the West Indies, she initiated the establishment of the University's Reggae Studies Unit which has hosted numerous fora, symposia and conferences on reggae, including the Global Reggae Conference convened in 2008. Her work has generated renewed interest in the fields of Cultural Studies, Gender Studies, Caribbean Studies, Languages and Literature.

Claude McKay OJ – World Renowned poet, journalist and author of several novels and anthologies.

Cyril Everard Palmer – Prolific author of children's books set in the Jamaican countryside, he received high praise for the excellence of his craftsmanship and sympathetic humour. In 1977 he was awarded the Silver Musgrave Medal for Literature from the Institute of Jamaica.

Edward Baugh – prolific writer, poet and actor who has a long list of publications to his credit.

Evan Jones - He moved to London in 1956 and established himself as a poet, novelist, playwright and screenwriter. His works often address social issues and war, though he is also well known in Jamaica as a children's writer. In Britain he is an Academy Award nominated screenwriter whose works include The Madhouse of Castle Street (1963), King and Country (1964), and the seminal television documentary series The Fight against Slavery (1975).

James Berry, OBE – Poet and author who settled in England in the 1940s. His poetry is notable for using a mixture of English and Jamaican Patois. He also wrote poetry collections for children, including When I Dance (1988), winner of the 1989 Signal Poetry Award; His collections of short stories earned him a Smarties Grand Prix Award and a Coretta Scott King Book Award (USA).

Kelly Magnus - Jamaican children's book author. Her most recent work was a series of children's books and parents' manuals that was part of a multimedia program called Max and Friends and that was specially designed for children with autism and related developmental disabilities.

Mervyn Morris OM – Poet and critic whose work appears widely in Caribbean, Commonwealth and British publications. Since the late 1960s he has built a solid reputation as a literary critic and essayist as well as one of Jamaica's leading poets.

Nalo Hopkinson – Writer and editor residing in Canada. Her science fiction, **fantasy** novels and short stories such as those in her collection Skin Folk often draw on **Caribbean** history and language, and its traditions of oral and written storytelling.

Nicole Dennis-Benn - Jamaican novelist. Her award-winning novel, Here Comes the Sun, was named a "Best Book of the year" by the New York Times and others. Her writing has been awarded a Richard and Julie Logsdon Fiction Prize; and two of her stories have been nominated for the prestigious Pushcart Prize in Fiction.

Orlando Patterson OD – Public intellectual, historical and cultural sociologist. He is the author of numerous academic papers and five major academic books including, Slavery and Social Death (1982); Freedom in the Making of Western Culture (1991); and The Ordeal of Integration (1997).

Pamela Claire Mordecai – Her poems and stories for children are widely known and have been used in textbooks in the UK, Canada, the USA, West Africa and the Caribbean. Her short stories have been published in journals and anthologies in the Caribbean, the USA and Canada.

Trevor Dave Rhone CD – Writer and Playwright. Among his works is the script to The Harder They Come - a 1972 crime film, which was instrumental in popularizing reggae in the US. He was awarded 3rd place of the top 100 all time black screen icons in the past 100 years.

Velma Pollard – Poet and fiction writer. Among her most noteworthy works are Shame Trees Don't Grow Here (1991) and Leaving Traces (2007). She is known for the melodious and expressive mannerisms in her work. She has published several anthologies and five poetry books. Her novel Karl won the Casa de las Americas literary prize in 1992.

Victor Stafford Reid OJ – Author of first West Indian novel to be written in dialect form. His works have become standard text books for black studies in Jamaica, the Caribbean, England and North America.

THE ARTS

– *Music*

Beenie Man (born Anthony Moses Davis) – Had his first number one single in 1993 in Jamaica and won DJ of the Year Award the same year, the first of eight consecutive awards. He has received an impressive number of international music awards including a MOBO Award for Best International Reggae Act in 1998. He has been featured in Newsweek and other major media outlets.

Beresford Hammond – Specialist in romantic lovers rock, although he has also delved into light dancehall, conscious roots reggae, hip-hop fusion, and straight-up contemporary R&B.

Bounty Killer (born Rodney Basil Price) - Is a Jamaican reggae and dancehall deejay. In 2002, collaboration with No Doubt, the song Hey Baby, won Bounty Killer his first Grammy Award, for Best Pop Vocal Performance by a duo or group. The deejay was also voted 'Guinness greatest Dancehall icon' in 2012 and later won deejay of the year in 2013.

Buju Banton (born Mark Anthony Myrie) – One of the most popular dancehall, **ragga**, and **reggae** musician who also recorded **Pop** and **Dance** songs, as well as songs dealing with **political** topics.

Bunny Wailer (born Neville O'Riley Livingston) – Singer, songwriter and percussionist he was an original member of reggae group *The Wailers*. He is widely regarded as a musical legend and is considered one of the long-time standard bearers of reggae music. He won the Grammy Award for Best Reggae Album in 1990, 1994 and 1996.

Byron Lee – **Musician**, record producer, and entrepreneur, best known for his work as leader of **Byron Lee and the Dragonaires.** He played a crucial pioneering role in bringing Jamaican music to the world. As a promoter and studio owner, he was instrumental in increasing the popularity of Jamaican music in the 1960s and 1970s.

Dalton Harris – Became the first foreign contestant to be crowned the winner of the of the UK X Factor competition in the 2018 series. His debut single, The Power of Love has topped the iTunes charts, beating out the likes of Ariana Grande, Halsey and Lady Gaga & Bradley Cooper.

Dean Fraser – Saxophonist who has contributed to hundreds of reggae recordings since the mid-1970s.

Dennis Brown – One of the most talented musicians of our time and has worked with virtually every one of the noted producers of contemporary reggae and ska. "The Crown Prince of Reggae" was one of the major stars of lovers rock, a sub-genre of reggae. Jamaica afforded Brown one of its highest honors - burial in the National Heroes Park in Kingston.

Diana King – Re**ggaefusion singer-songwriter** who specifically performed a mixture and fusion of **R&B, reggae, pop** and **dancehall.**

Eric Donaldson – Singer songwriter who could be regarded as the "King of Festival" having won the song competition five times. His winning 1971 entry, "Cherry Oh Baby", launched him into the limelight and his patriotic "Land of my Birth" and "Sweet Jamaica" are favourites especially among the Jamaican Diaspora.

Freddie McGregor – Singer, songwriter and producer with a career spanning over than forty years. He has toured extensively headlining international concerts around the world.

Gregory Isaacs – One of Jamaica's most beloved vocalists whose career has stretched over 30 years. From the heady days of reggae through lover's rock, a genre he helped develop, his talent reached into the modern age and produced albums such as "Night Nurse", which was a huge international success.

Jessica Yap – an extraordinarily gifted violinist who at only seven years old became both the youngest Jamaican to perform with an orchestra and the youngest in the Caribbean to get a Distinction in the Grade Five theory Associated Board of the Royal Schools of Music (ABRSM) exam. At 13 years old Yap earned the diploma ABRSM, and at 16, she achieved the Licentiate of The Royal Schools of Music (LRSM). She is the region's youngest violinist to get either award, or the youngest violinist in the hemisphere to complete all the ABRSM grades.

Jimmy Cliff (born James Chambers) – Musician, Actor, singer, songwriter, music producer and businessman. Jimmy Cliff whose career has spanned approximately 50 years was inducted into the Rock and Roll Hall of Fame in 2010. He is also the recipient of Jamaica's third highest honour – the Order of Merit.

Lloyd Lovindeer – A versatile and talented dancehall deejay who for some thirty years has used witty and satirical lyrics to commentate on grievous situations or realities of the day. He also scored with a number of soca albums.

Marion Hall (Lady Saw) – Reggae singer, known as "the First Lady of Dancehall". She is the first female **deejay** to win a Grammy Award and to be certified a triple -platinum artist. She is also the first woman to headline dancehall shows outside her native Jamaica.

Mutabaruka (born Allan Hope) – Helped to forge an entirely new genre of music, dub/rhythm poetry. He focuses on social justice, human rights and black liberation. He has performed his work all over the world and released several outstanding albums of dub poetry.

Peter Tosh (born Winston Hubert McIntosh) – Reggae musician, songwriter, composer and core member of the Wailers, his music was infused with political morality, social issues and social messages and he went on to have a successful solo career. As a songwriter, Tosh contributed many of the Wailers hits. His skilful guitar playing and vocal skills were also central to the band's sound.

Robert Nesta "Bob" Marley – Singer-songwriter and musician. He remains the most widely known and revered performer of reggae music and is credited for helping spread both Jamaican music and the **Rastafari movement** to a worldwide audience.

Sean Paul Ryan Francis Henriques (Sean Paul) – dancehall rapper, singer and record producer. Most of his albums have been nominated for the Grammy's Best Reggae Album, with Dutty Rock winning the award. He has had chart topping songs in the United States and has been featured in many other chart topping singles.

Shabba Ranks (born Rexton Gordon) – One of the most popular dancehall **recording artist** and one of the first deejays to gain international acceptance and break into the mainstream music industry.

Shaggy (born Orville Richard Burrell) – Reggae singer and philanthropist with a baritone singing voice. His major hits include; "Oh Carolina", "Boombastic", "It Wasn't Me" and "Angel. Shaggy started his philanthropy, as a project called Shaggy and Friendz, in 2016, donating over US$1 million, to the Bustamante Children's Hospital in Jamaica.

Tessanne Amanda Chin - Recording artist, best known for winning Season 5 of NBC's reality TV singing competition The Voice. She has opened for famous acts such as Patti Labelle, Peabo Bryson and Gladys Knight. In 013, Tessanne was named Caribbean Journal's 2013 Artist of the Year.

Willard White – One of the world's great basses, known for his enormous rich voice and powerful stage presence. Grammy-winning opera singer who appeared as the soloist at the opening ceremony of the Millennium Dome in London. His large repertoire includes bass-baritone roles in operas my Monteverdi, Handel, Mozart, Prokofiev and Gershwin, and he has worked with the London Philharmonic, La Scala Orchestra, the Berlin Philharmonic and Los Angeles Philharmonic.

Yellowman (born Winston Foster) – Dancehall Deejay and Reggae Artist popular in Jamaica in the 1980s, coming to prominence with a series of singles that established his reputation. One of the widest-touring artists in the reggae industry, he is massively popular in Nigeria, **Peru, Sweden, Italy, Germany, England, France, Kenya** and the **United States.**

Black Uhuru – Formed in 1972, initially as Uhuru (Swahili for 'freedom'). The group has undergone several line-up changes over the years, and had their most successful period in the 1980s, with their album *Anthem* winning the first ever Grammy Award for Best Reggae Album in 1985.

Boney M – Jamaican born Lead singer Liz Mitchell and Vocalist Marcia Barrett were the two original members of the band that did most of their studio recordings. The band has sold more than 80 million records and is known for huge international hits such as "Daddy Cool", "Ma Baker", "Sunny", "Rasputin", "Mary's Boy Child – Oh My Lord" and "Rivers of Babylon".

Byron Lee and the Dragonaires – a **ska, calypso** and **soca** band which played a crucial pioneering role in bringing Caribbean music to the **world**. Formed in 1956 and playing a big band-ska sound their big break came in the first James Bond film, Dr. No, where they appeared as the band in the scene at Pussfeller's club and played a number of tunes on the soundtrack.

The I-threes – A trio featuring Marcia Griffiths, **Rita Marley**, and **Judy Mowatt**, the I-Threes provided the rich harmonies for Bob Marley's performances and recordings from 1974 until his death. Although they continued to perform together following Marley's death, they later pursued solo careers.

Third World – Formed in 1973 Third World is one of the top Reggae bands of all time producing and performing positive, progressive and internationally relevant music. The band combines Jamaican Reggae and Folk music with strains of African Rhythms, American Pop, Rhythm & Blues, Rap and Classical music. Third World is one of the longest running and most diverse bands Jamaica has ever produced.

Toots and the Maytals – Considered legends of ska and reggae music, their sound is a unique combination of gospel, ska, soul, reggae and rock. The group was featured in one of reggae's greatest breakthrough events The Harder They Come, the 1972 film and soundtrack starring Jimmy Cliff. The band won the 2005 Grammy award for best reggae album - True Love, an album consisting of re-recorded versions of their classics.

Lowell Dunbar **(Sly) & Robert Shakespeare (Robbie)** – One of **reggae's** most prolific and long lasting production teams. Their rhythms have been the driving force behind innumerable songs. As a production team, the pair has been the equivalent of a creative storm, the cutting edge of modern dub, ragga, and dancehall.

THE ARTS

– Performing Arts

Basil Wallace – Possibly best known for his breakthrough appearance as Screwface, Stephen Segal's ruthless co-star in "Marked for Death". He also appeared in Blood Diamond, Joy Ride and Free Willy 2. For television, he has been in episodes of West Wing, Judging Amy, The Pretender, Any Day Now, and NYPD Blue.

Bobby Ghisays – Well known director, actor, and television host who directed three pantomimes - "Johnny Reggae", The Pirate Princess" and "Ginneral B". He covered everything from opera to drama, musicals to melodrama and revues to comedies and appeared in several films. He also directed television commercials and radio jingles. In 1980 he was invited by Black Theatre Canada to direct Lorraine Hansberry's classic "Raisin in the Sun". Previously in 1976, he had been invited to co-write and direct the revue "Bathurst Street.". He died in 1990.

Carl Bradshaw – Talented award-winning actor and director who came to fame in the critically acclaimed Jamaican movie The Harder They Come. He starred in numerous films including Smile Orange, Countryman, Dance Hall Queen, Mighty Quinn (with Denzil Washington), Club Paradise (with Robin Williams and Jimmy Cliff), among others. He produced video and TV shows such as Miami Vice, and co-produced Dancehall Queen, in which he plays a supporting role.

Charles Hyatt – Actor, playwright, director and comedian who appeared in numerous films and television shows beginning in the 1960s. After making his movie debut in the 1965 film *A High Wind in Jamaica* he had notable performances in the films Crossplot, Club Paradise, The Mighty Quinn, Cool Runnings and Almost Heaven. He also appeared in the hilarious movie Smile Orange.

Paul Campbell – Popular actor who is best known for starring in films such as Dancehall Queen, Third World Cop and Shottas. In addition to these roles, he has also acted on stage in Jamaica and on Broadway in New York City.

Reggie Carter – Actor, journalist and advertising executive who appeared in the "The Lunatic", "Royal Palm Estate" and in the James Bond film "Dr. No". He is rated as one of the island's leading actors and also as a founding father of Jamaican advertising. He died in 1995.

Leonie Forbes – Actress, announcer, producer and presenter who played leading roles in twelve pantomimes and acted in plays such as: Sea Mama; The Rope and the Cross; Old Story Time; and Champagne and Sky Juice. She also appeared in films such as: Children of Babylon; Club Paradise; The Orchid House; Milk and Honey; What My Mother Told Me and Soul Survivor (1995)

Madge Sinclair – In 1978 starred in the movie Convoy as the Widow Maker. She would later receive an Emmy Award nomination for her role as Belle in the mini-series Roots. In 1988, Sinclair played Queen Aoleon in the comedy, Coming to America. She also had roles in The Lion King, Star Trek and received an Emmy award for her role in the series Gabriel's Fire.

Olive Lewin – Over 200 of Jamaica's folk songs were composed by Dr Olive Lewin, founder of the Jamaica Folk Singers, musicologist and author. She has done audio and videotapes on Jamaican folk music and gained national and international recognition for her contribution to Jamaican culture. Dr Lewin has earned a Musgrave medal, Order of Jamaica, Commander of the Order of Distinction, Licentiate of the Royal School of Music, Licentiate of the Royal Academy of Music, Licentiate of the Trinity College of Music, Fellow Trinity College of Music and Associate of the Royal College of Music.

Oliver Samuels – Actor and Comedian often described as the Jamaican "King of Comedy" performing both stand up and comic theatre. He became extremely popular on the Jamaica Broadcasting Corporation's television series Oliver At Large and Several spin-off theatre pieces have been created for the Oliver character including Large Abroad, Oliver's Posse (1999), Oliver and Pinocchio (2001), and Oliver and the Genie (2002). He has appeared in the films: The Mighty Quinn, Countryman and Smile Orange. He frequently tours Britain and North America.

Peter Williams – Actor currently residing in Canada. The majority of his work has been in television, including the role of the primary villain Apophis in the first four seasons of *Stargate SG-1*. He recently played the lead Gene Wright in Frances-Anne Solomon's 2007 feature film A Winter Tale.

Raina Simone Moore – Jamaican-born actress who guest starred on ABC's Boston Legal. She has also co-starred on "All of Us" the CW 11 sitcom, produced by Will Smith and Jada Pinkett. She appeared in over a dozen-theatre ensemble as well as national commercials for McDonald's and Wendy's.

Rex Nettleford – Scholar, social critic, choreographer, trade union educator, author, university vice-chancellor, dancer, choreographer and visionary. In 1963 he founded the National Dance Theatre Company of Jamaica, an ensemble which under his direction did much to incorporate traditional Jamaican music and dance into a formal balletic repertoire. He was also the artistic director for the **University Singers** of the University of the West Indies for over twenty years.

Rondolph Samuel Williams (Mass Ran/Ranny) – Dramatist, comedian and television personality who did his first pantomime "Bluebeard and Brer Anancy" in 1942. His outstanding achievement in the field of entertainment and drama earned him several awards. The Ranny Williams Entertainment Centre stands as a monument to his work.

Roxanne Beckford (a.k.a. Roxanne Beckford-Hoge) - Is an American actress who was born and raised in Jamaica. She has acted in numerous television series and played small roles in movies, including Bewitched (2005) Something's Gotta Give (2003), and Father of the Bride Part II (1995). Beckford began her career in acting as a child starring in television commercials in Jamaica.

THE ARTS
– Visual Arts

Jamaica has a long history in the film industry; Palm Pictures studio, headed by Chris Blackwell is behind the production of many Jamaican movies. The island's natural beauty makes Jamaica a favourite location for filming. The Jamerican Film and Music Festival, a four-day annual festival takes place in Montego Bay in November. Films shot in whole or in part in Jamaica include:

Treasure Island (1950)
A High Wind in Jamaica (1965)
20,000 Leagues Under the Sea (1954)
Dr. No (1962)
Hammerhead (1968)
The Harder They Come (1973)
Live and Let Die (1973)
Papillon (1973)
Blue Lagoon (1980)
Eureka (1981)
Club Paradise (1986)
Clara's Heart (1988)
Cocktail (1988)
The Mighty Quinn (1989)
Marked for Death (1990)
Lord of the Flies (1990)
Treasure Island (1990 film)
Piranha II: The Spawning (1990)
Popcorn (1991 film)
Going to Extremes (1992)
The Lunatic (1992)
Prelude to a Kiss (1992)
Cool Runnings (1993)
Wide Sargasso Sea (1993)
Scam (1993)
Klash (1994)
The House Next Door (1995)
Dancehall Queen (1997)
How Stella Got Her Groove Back (1998)
Instict (1998)
Third World Cop (2000)
Shottas (2002)
One Love (2003)

BEAUTY AND MODELING

Miss (Jamaica) World Beauty Queens

1963 - Joan Crawford   1976 - Cindy Breakspeare   1993 - Lisa Hanna

International Models

Althea Laing – Pioneered modeling in Jamaica and was the Caribbean's first model to appear on the cover of the international magazine Essence. She also appeared in a movie "Daughters of the Dust" in Atlanta.

Brandon Bailey - Made his debut modelling on the Prada runway in Milan, Italy, in 2015. He went on to make runway appearances for Paul Smith, Berluti and Yeezy, in addition to featuring in an ad campaign for Ralph Lauren.

Canise Jackson – Also known as 'CJ,' Jackson was the first black model to grace the cover of a Singapore magazine, Lookbook, in 2003. The Saint star has also covered French Divas magazine, appeared in campaigns for Giorgio Armani, Carven, Gattinoni, Collezioni and more; and has also done editorials for Italian Vogue, Shape Magazine and more. She has also appeared in Bravo's The Fashion Show.

Carla Campbel – Appeared in the 2006 Sports Illustrated Swimsuit Issue; only the second Caribbean model to do Victoria's Secret campaign.

Grace Jones – Model, singer and actress. She has appeared in many mainstream films such as the 1984 film "Conan the Destroyer" the 1985 James Bond movie A View to a Kill and the 1992 Eddie Murphy film Boomerang. She has also recorded several albums which have generated success in different markets.

Jaunel McKenzie - Jaunel is the first Caribbean-born model in history to be ranked the number one black model in the world by Models.com. The Jamaican-born model was discovered by Pulse at the age of 16 during their very first Caribbean model search in 2002. McKenzie has built an enviable portfolio, with multiple spreads in Vogue – 11 for American Vogue and one each for the German, French, and Italian editions.

Karin Taylor – Chosen by Playboy as their Playmate of the Month - June 1996. She has also appeared on Malcolm and Eddie, Weird Al Show, Keenan Ivory Wayans Show, Baywatch and as a guest host on entertainment television.

Kimberly Mais Issa – Mais became the Caribbean's first global supermodel, becoming a star in the Asian, US and European markets. She created history in 1987 when she beat out more than 1,000 Japanese and international models to become the face of

Japan's Kirin beer campaign. In Europe, she appeared on magazine covers, commercials and editorials across the continent, including a spread for French Cosmopolitan. She was even the face of Turkey's Tourism campaign in 1988.

Nadine Willis – Graced the pages of British and French Vogue and was the first black woman to do a Gucci campaign.

Oraine Barrett – Barrett is one of the most famous homegrown male model the Caribbean has ever produced. He modelled for Abercrombie & Fitch, John Bartlett and Pepe Jeans, before going on to become the face of Ralph Lauren. He has appeared on the cover of GQ, and in editorials in i-D, Interview, Vogue Hommes Japan, Arena Homme, Italian Vogue and more

Sanya Hughes – Hughes won the Miss Jamaica Universe title in 2002, and she utilised her popularity to create a successful international modelling career. Her resume includes a campaign for Bare Minerals), Selfridges in London and other major UK department stores; national ads for Honda, Budweiser and Corona (US) and being specially selected for the role of Mermaid in Pirates of the Caribbean.

Stacey McKenzie – Fashion model whose magazine covers include Essence, **Le Monde** and Panache, as well as editorials in **Vogue** (US, Japan, Korean, British, Spanish), Harper's Bazaar, **Interview, Flare**, Fashion, and Vibe Magazine. She has also appeared as a judge on the TV show Canada's Next Top Model.

BUSINESS

Ann-Marie Campbell – Campbell is the executive vice-president at the Home Depot Stores. This means she is in charge of approximately 2,000 stores in the United States. She has received numerous honours, including being named to Fortune's 2014 and 2016 list of 50 Most Powerful Women in Business. She was Fortune Magazine 16th most powerful woman in the world of business for 2018.

Audrey Hinchcliffe - This Jamaican businesswoman is head of Manpower and Maintenance Services Ltd. She was also invited by former United States Secretary of State Hillary Clinton to join the US Department of State's International Council on Women's Business Leadership for a two-year term. Hinchcliffe is principal of Caribbean Health Management Consultants Limited.

Audrey Marks – regarded as one of Jamaica's most powerful business leaders and entrepreneurs, her vision gave birth to Jamaica's first multi-service bill-payment chain, Paymaster Jamaica Limited. She is also the first female president of the American Chamber of Commerce of Jamaica.

Basil Johnson - Founder and managing director of Montego Bay-based Discount Lumber & Hardware Limited, Discount Lumber Limited, and Discount Mart Limited. He is a self-made businessman and has for many years provided employment to many persons in the west.

Chris Blackwell - President and CEO of Island Records and Palm Pictures. He established himself as a music mogul more than 50 years ago. His rise included introducing the world to reggae. He produced music for artists like Ike and Tina Turner, Bob Marley and the Wailers, Burning Spear and Black Uhuru, among others. He is also the founder of Palm Pictures and creator of the Golden Eye Film Festival that honors Jamaicans who excel in the arts and music.

Don Wehby - Chief executive officer of Grace Kennedy. He's known as a quick thinker and has been making big gains for that company since he took on the top job.

Donna Duncan-Scott - She has been the managing director of Jamaica Money Market Brokers Ltd since 1998 and serves as its group executive director of culture and human development. She is also a qualified engineer.

Earl Jarrett - General manager of Jamaica National Building Society (JNBS) since October 1999. He joined the society in May 1997. He is also chairman of the JNBS Foundation, the Jamaica Automobile Association (Services) Ltd, JN Overseas (US) Inc, JN Overseas (UK) Limited, and JN Overseas (Canada) Limited.

Fred Smith - Managing director of Tropical Tours and Exclusive Holidays Limited. He has excelled in the tourism ground-transportation business. Smith has operated and managed his companies well, allowing him to be among the leading businessmen in Montego Bay and, by extension, western Jamaica

Gary 'Butch' Hendrickson - Chairman and chief executive officer of National Baking Company and Coconut Bay Beach Resort & Spa. He was among the first to introduce biodegradable polyethylene packaging for his products. He also reduced the sugar content of some popular products long before the low-sugar campaign was launched. He has received numerous awards including the Jamaica Observer Business Leader Award.

Glen Christian - Chairman and founder of Cari-Med and Kirk Distributors. His experience spans more than 40 years working in the pharmaceutical and fast-moving consumer goods industries. Cari-Med boasts a staff compliment of 380 and is one of the leading pharmaceutical companies in the Caribbean.

Gordon Butch Stewart – Chairman of over two dozen companies throughout the Caribbean, North America and Great Britain. These companies include: Sandals Resorts Beaches Family Resorts, Appliance Traders, Ltd. and The Jamaica Observer.

Jacqueline Sharp - President and chief executive officer of Scotiabank. Her appointment to the top job was historic, as she was the bank's first female boss. It also made Scotia Group the only stock market company with both a female chairman and CEO.

John Joseph Issa – Chairman of the Super Clubs Super-Inclusive resorts chain and vice-chairman of the Gleaner Company, Mr. Issa is credited with introducing the all-inclusive concept into Jamaica some thirty years ago.

Joseph M. Matalon (Matalon family) – Chairman and chief executive officer of the ICD Group. Once a major industrial empire, the ICD Group has now been restructured and reoriented.

Karl Hendrickson - He is the founder of the National baking empire, which has expanded over the years and now includes business interests in the hotel and agro-processing sectors. The family businesses which he started employ more than 4,000 persons.

Kenny Benjamin – Founder and Chairman of Guardsman Security. The Guardsman Group of Companies includes thousands of private security personnel; tourism and technological interests; a botanical garden, zoo and family playground; and vast real estate holdings.

Kingsley Cooper – Credited with pioneering the billion-dollar Pulse Investments Ltd in Jamaica and launching the careers of several international models, he effected a number of innovations and firsts for Jamaica and the wider Caribbean. These included the Caribbean Model Search, an international modelling agency,

Caribbean Fashion Week, the Superjam concert series, the lifestyle television programme Caribbean Fashion Weekly and the region's new fashion reality TV show - The Search for the Caribbean's Next Supermodel.

Lascelles Chin – Lasco's Chairman and CEO now heads one of the leading manufacturers and distributors of pharmaceuticals, food and drink in Jamaica. The corporate entity provides hundreds of products to Jamaica, the Caribbean, Latin America, North America and England.

Michael Lee Chin – Amongst other positions, he is currently Executive Chairman of AIC Limited (a Canadian mutual fund), and the National Commercial Bank of Jamaica. In the latest Forbes Billionaires List, he was placed at number 701, with assets worth around $1 billion.

Patrick Adams – Gourmet chef and caterer with a host of international clients that include Diddy, Russell Simmons, Donald Trump, Mike Tyson, Shaquille O'Neal, Tiger Woods, and others. Adams has also catered at one of former United States President Barack Obama's re-election fund-raisers while he was the sitting President.

Phillip Gore - Executive chairman of Gore Developments. He has received many awards for his work in shaping the construction industry and for contributing to the economic development of Jamaica. He is also well known for charity work.

Richard Azan – Chief Executive Officer of Ralaica Trading Company in Central Kingston which wholesales a wide range of products including household items, clothing, shoes and toys.

Rita Humphries-Lewin – One of the first women in the Western Hemisphere to bridge the barrier of becoming a stockbroker back in the early '60s. She is the founder and chairman of Barita Group of Companies, which includes Barita Investments Ltd, Barita Portfolio Management Limited and the Barita Unit Trusts Management Company Ltd, and BPM Financial. She was the chairman of the Jamaica Stock Exchange from 1998 to 2000 and during her tenure, she established the Central Securities Depository. From 2001 to 2006, she was the chairman of Development Bank of Jamaica.

Thalia Lyn – Founder and Chief Executive Officer of Island Grill, a chain of fast food restaurants which transformed traditional

Jamaica jerk into a major restaurant chain with locations in Jamaica and Barbados. She earned many awards including Business Leader of the Year from the Florida International University MSBA Class of 2002 and the company received the Best Fast Food Award in 1998.

Wayne Chen – Chief Executive Officer of Super Plus Food Stores, a large supermarket chain with at least 30 outlets across the island.

LAW

Alayne Frankson-Wallace – a Jamaican-born attorney, and former judge was appointed executive director of the Office of Administration of Justice at the United Nations (UN) in 2017. She has over 23 years of legal experience at the national and international levels, including in the internal justice system at the United Nations. Earlier in her career, Frankson-Wallace prosecuted people accused of the most serious violations of international humanitarian law as prosecuting counsel at the United Nations International Criminal Tribunal for Rwanda (2005-2008).

Amardo Wesley Pitters - The first black lawyer to have served in the Alabama Court of Civil Appeals. He was born in St. Ann's Bay Jamaica and attended University of Alabama School of Law in Tuscaloosa, Alabama where he obtained a Juris Doctorate. After serving on Alabama's appellate court he went into private practice with the law firm Terry G. Davis, P.C. in Montgomery, Alabama. During his years with the firm he represented, among other clients, Alabama State University, Alabama Education Association, and Alabama Democratic Conference.

Barbara Lee - Jamaican-born attorney appointed in 2015 to serve as a judge at Buffalo City Court. The Jamaican native attended Canisius College and received a BA in Philosophy from SUNY at Buffalo in 1981 and her Juris Doctorate from State University of New York at Buffalo Law School in 1986. While in law school, she served on the law school admissions committee and was elected vice-president of the Black Law Students Association. She was admitted to the New York State Bar in 1991.

Claudia Gordon - The first deaf student to graduate from the American University's Washington College of Law. Gordon was appointed by the Obama administration to serve as White House's disability liaison to oversee its efforts on disability issues between the administration and the disability community. She has worked for the National Association of the Deaf Law and Advocacy Centre as well as the US Department of Homeland Security.

Dahlia A. Walker-Huntington – Family Law and County Court Mediator, a Certified Arbitrator, Special Magistrate for the City of Miramar and the Broward County Animal Court, trial attorney and radio commentator. She is also a consultant for the Ministry of Foreign Affairs on the Jamaica Diaspora project for Southern United States.

Dudley J. Thompson – Lawyer, Ambassador, Pan-Africanist, Politician and Statesman practised as a Barrister-at law in East Africa- including Tanganyika and Kenya and was part of the international legal team that defended Jomo Kenyatta.

Edward Zacca – The former Chief Justice of Jamaica was the fourth Caribbean Chief Justice to be appointed to Britain's Privy Council and the first from Jamaica. He also served in the Courts of Appeal in Bermuda, Turks and Caicos Islands and the Cayman Islands. He was knighted by Britain's Queen Elizabeth in 2015.

Heather Victoria Rabbatts - Jamaican-born British solicitor, businesswoman, and broadcaster, who rose to prominence as Chief executive of the London Borough of Lambeth, the youngest council chief in the UK. She served as a Football Association director from 2011 to 2017 and was the first ethnic minority person to do so. She was also the only woman on its board.

Jerry Hamilton - is a board-certified civil trial lawyer who has received national recognition as one of the Top Ten Defence Lawyers in the United States by one of the biggest insurance firms in the world. He is a Fellow of the Litigation Counsel of America, which is an invitation-only trial honorary society whose members represent less than one-half percent of lawyers in the US. He is also board-certified in maritime law and has been recognized as a "Super Lawyer" by Law & Politics every year since 2006.

Jewel C. Scot – A graduate of the Norman Manley Law School she made history in 2005 when she simultaneously became the first female and first Caribbean-American District Attorney for Clayton County, Atlanta, Georgia by defeating District Attorney Bob Keller who held the position for 27 years. She is the recipient of numerous community awards for Leadership on Women, children's and youth issues and the author of the book "Portrait of a Woman", 1998.

Kenneth Rattray – Accomplished diplomat and an eminent jurist in the international community on issues relating to the United Nations Convention on the Law of the Sea, the International Seabed Authority, and the International Civil Aviation Organisation. The 32nd Edward Warner Award, the highest honour in the world of civil aviation, was conferred by the Council of the International Civil Aviation Organization (ICAO) on him in recognition of his eminent contribution to the development of international civil aviation, particularly in the legal field.

Lloyd George Barnett – Commonwealth Human Rights Advocate. His doctoral thesis on the evolution and adaptation of responsible government in Jamaica which was accepted by the University of London in 1966, was subsequently published under the title "Constitutional Law of Jamaica" and remains the definitive text on the subject. He published several learned articles and written countless papers on varying areas of law.

Margaret Ramsay-Hale – In 2014 she was sworn in as the first female chief justice of the Turks and Caicos Islands (TCI). Justice Ramsay-Hale holds a degree in economics from the London School of Economics in addition to her law degree from the University of the West Indies. Prior to her arrival in the Turks and Caicos Islands she was appointed a judge of the Family Court in St James, Jamaica, eventually moving to the criminal courts as a resident magistrate for the parish

Neville Noel Ashenheim – (18 Dec 1900-1 Sept 1984) Businessman, lawyer, politician, who served as the first Jamaican Ambassador to the **United States.** He received a knighthood from **Queen Elizabeth II** on 1 January 1963.

Patrick Robinson – elected President of the International Criminal Tribunal for the Former Yugoslavia by fellow judges on 4 November 2008 and re-elected in October 2009. He was first elected as a judge of the Tribunal by the UN General Assembly in October 1998 and has since been re-elected twice. In 2004, he presided over the trial of former Yugoslav president Slobodan Milošević the first former head of state to be tried for war crimes.

Patrick Rousseau – He was an eminent Lawyer with a distinguished career in business and public service. Known as an adept business negotiator, he had leadership roles on several company boards across several sectors such as construction, manufacturing, insurance, finance, entertainment, education, and heath. He played a major role in the building of Myers, Fletcher & Gordon to a legal conglomerate of international recognition and his legal prowess helped to attract foreign capital and stimulate local business interests to engage in corporate enterprises for Jamaica's economic growth.

Ramon Alberga – Queen's Counsel, former Vice President of the Jamaican Law Society, Past President of the Cayman Islands Law Society and Consulting Editor of the Cayman Islands Law Reports. He served the judiciary for some 50 years and received an OBE for long and significant contribution to the development of jurisprudence in the Cayman Islands. He served as vice-president of the Jamaican Bar Association, and assisted in steering the way forward as the separation of the roles and functions of solicitors and barristers was abandoned.

Renatha Francis – In 2018 she was appointed to the Eleventh Judicial Circuit Court by Govenor Rick Scott,. She previously practiced with Shutts & Bowen, LLP, and served as an attorney for the First District Court of Appeal. Renatha migrated from Jamaica where she attended St. Hugh's High and Bridgeport Primary school. She received her bachelor's degree from the University of the West Indies and her law degree from Florida Coastal Law School in 2010.

Richard E. Myers – Professor at the University of North California School of Law. He was a federal prosecutor in both California and North Carolina where he prosecuted a variety of crimes ranging from counterfeiting to firearms and narcotics. In 2019 he was nominated for a Federal Judge Post in the Eastern District of North Carolina.

Stephen Vasciannie – Former Deputy Solicitor-General and principal of the Norman Manley Law School, Vasciannie served as Jamaica's Ambassador Extraordinary Plenipotentiary to the United States from 2012 up to July 17, 2015. He previously worked as a Legal Advisor at the United Nations Centre on Transnational Corporations. In 2006, he was elected to serve for five years on the United Nations International Law Commission and in 2011 elected for a second term.

SCIENCE AND MEDICINE

Abraham Anthony Chen – Professor of Applied Atmospheric Physics in the Department of Physics and former Head of the Climate Studies Group, one of the leading centres for climate change research in the Caribbean. He was a member of the Intergovernmental Panel on Climate Change which shared the 2007 Nobel Prize with former US Vice President, Mr. Al Gore.

Amza Ali (Dr) – Senior consultant neurologist, founder and president of the Jamaican League Against Epilepsy and medical director of the Epilepsy Centre of Jamaica. Dr. Ali has been recognised by the American Academy of Neurology (AAN) for his work in the field of epilepsy in Jamaica and the English-speaking Caribbean. The award positioned Jamaica as the only country in the region to have obtained such prestigious recognition from the AAN.**Anthony Vendryes (Dr.)** – Physician and author of the book "An Ounce of Prevention" was engaged in transforming his medical practice to holistic and integrative medicine which combines both conventional and alternative based modalities. He strongly promoted prevention and healthy lifestyles through his popular weekly radio programme, newspaper column and through various health and wellness lectures, seminars and workshops.

Austin James Thomas – Introduced an approach to the selection of fish which was immensely successful, and which spawned successful industries in many countries including the USA, countries in Africa and Israel.

Basil Waine Kong (Dr.) – Former CEO of the Association of Black Cardiologists Dr. Kong has been at the forefront of efforts to reduce the ravages of heart disease, diabetes and stroke. He partnered with Dr Elijah Saunders to conduct the first clinical trials for African Americans relating to high blood pressure. In 1978, they developed language describing the early warning signs of heart attack which was later adopted by the American Heart Association. They also authored the Vital Signs Quality of Life questionnaire that was used in several clinical trials.

Bert Fraser-Reid (Professor) – Synthetic organic chemist and world renowned researcher has been widely recognized for his work using carbohydrates as starting materials for chiral materials and on the role of oligosaccharides in immune response.

Carron Gordon (Dr), Professors Rainford Wilks and Affette McCaw-Binns, - Medical researchers at the University of the West Indies have made a breakthrough discovery in treating patients who have suffered a stroke. The five-year study published in 2013 under the title Community Based Walking after Stroke. The findings have generated widespread interest across the United States and have caused specialists to now rethink their approach in the treatment of stroke patients.

Cicely Delphine Williams (Dr.) – Paediatrician noted for her early description of and work with Kwashiorkor.

Diane Thompson (Dr.) – Director of Inpatient Rehabilation Unit at Columbia University Medical Centre. She is also an assistant professor of clinical medicine and rehabilitation and the author of two books.

Errol Morrison (Professor) - Endocrinologist and Biochemist who has changed the face of diabetes in Jamaica, the Caribbean and the world. His work is centered on the investigation of medicinal plants used in the treatment of diabetes mellitus. He has spearheaded major research and developmental activities related to diabetes care and management attracting major funding in the area.

Gavin O. Jones (Dr.) – He was named one of the world's top global thinkers. An IBM Q Ambassador and research staff member in the Quantum Applications in Chemistry and Science group at IBM Research he received an Outstanding Technical Achievement Award from IBM and was awarded an FP Global Thinkers Award: Innovator Category by Foreign Policy Magazine for his achievements in sustainability and recycling.

Gerald C. Lalor (Professor) – Environmental Geochemist- created a geochemical map of the elements in Jamaican soils and uncovered many previous unidentified elements which augers great benefits for the Jamaican society with significant applications to sectors such as agriculture, health and mineralogy.

Harold M. Johnson (Dr.) – Principal Medical Officer of health who successfully led the fight against hookworm, ringworm, and malaria in Jamaica.

Henry Lowe – **(Dr)** - World renowned scientist and leader in the field of medical research who has been researching plants indigenous to Jamaica for their bioactive properties, as well as their potential for pharmaceuticals, nutraceuticals and cosmeceuticals. He gained worldwide recognition after his research found that the Jamaican Ball Moss contains cancer-fighting properties and the anti-cancer compounds that they have extracted from the Jamaican Ball Moss have been demonstrated to kill prostate cancer and other cancer cells in vitro and in vivo. He has already developed nutraceuticals from the Ball Moss and other Jamaican plants. The US Food and Drug Administration (FDA) recently granted orphan drug approval for Chrysoeriol, a cannabis-based drug used to treat acute myeloid leukaemia, which also developed by Dr Lowe. In 2013 Dr Henry Lowe was honoured by the United States Government for his contributions to the sciences, science education and exemplary public service.

Herb Fitzgerald Sewell (Professor) – Has been a representative for the UK at the WHO Consultation on Xenotransplantation and a member of the UK regulatory authority overseeing developments in Xenotransplantation. A member of the Nuffield Council on Bioethics and is a Commissioner for the UK Medicines Commission and he was made a Founding Fellow of the UK Academy of Medical Sciences in 1999. He was awarded the honorary degrees of DDS by Birmingham University in 2001 and DSC by the University of the West Indies in 2003.

Jeff Palmer (Professor) – An international expert on barley and sorghum. In barley research he developed the abrasion process which accelerated the production process of malt. He published at least 150 scientific papers and compiled, wrote the major chapter, and edited probably the most important research book on barley called Cereal Science and Technology. In 1998 he was awarded the American Society of Brewing Chemist Award for distinction in research and good citizenship in science. He worked as a consultant for international brewers worldwide and is a fellow of the Institute of Biology and a Doctor of Science.

Keith Barrington Jones (Professor) - Jamaica's first virologist who formulated the typhoid vaccine in the 1950s and was also involved in the formulation of the polio vaccine

Kenneth Richards (Dr.) – Developed the "Richards Procedure" which made lung transplants feasible in humans.

Leigh D. Lord (Dr.) – Blood transfusion pioneer who also developed "Tia Maria", the world renowned coffee liquor.

Lloyd A. Dayes – Professor of Neurology, delivers motivational speeches to students around the world. He has been principal researcher in the areas of neurological and neuro-immunological diseases and is currently active in brain tumour research on the most malignant tumour of the brain - Glioblastoma Multiforme.

Louis Grant (Professor) – Microbiologist and Pathologist he created a mass vaccination for Tuberculosis in Jamaica. He also did ground-breaking work for diseases like Leptospirosis, Equine Encephalitis and Dengue Fever.

Manley West (Professor) and Albert Lockhart (Dr.) – conducted pioneering research that turned raw ganja into specialty medicines for glaucoma and other disorders. They created Canosol and later Cantimol which was the world's first combination of an alpha agonist and a beta blocker in one bottle which are necessary for glaucoma therapy and were previously delivered separately. In the early 1990s, they also developed the drug Asmasol, to treat asthma, colds and the flu.

Mercedes Dullum (Dr) – A specialist in cardiothoracic surgery based at the Cleveland Clinic in Florida. She was voted Washington's Top Cardiac Surgeon by Washington magazine, and in 2005, she was named Physician of the Year by the South Florida Business Journal. She has written 21 scientific papers on cardiac surgery and is a pioneer in the revolutionary 'off-pump' method of minimally invasive cardiac surgery. This means she uses a procedure that does not require cutting open a person's chest to get to the heart but instead making a small vertical incision in the sternum in order to carry out the procedure.

Neil Persadsingh (Dr.) – Leading dermatologist and author of the book "Acne in Black Women" and "The Hair in Black Women". He is a fellow of the American Academy of Dermatology and a foundation member of the Dermatological Association of Jamaica and the Caribbean Dermatological Association.

Patrice Smith – Professor of neuroscience in the psychology department at Carleton University and a research fellow at Harvard Medical School. She conducted ground breaking research which has major implications for the regeneration and repair of damaged nerves. The research hopes to provide novel effective therapies which will be specifically beneficial to those who suffer spinal cord injury, as well as those with brain injury and optic nerve injury.

Patricia DeLeon – Professor of biological sciences at the University of Delaware; she has been a visiting scientist at the Johns Hopkins University School of Medicine and the University of Pennsylvania School of Medicine, as well as an adjunct professor at Penn State University College of Medicine. A 1996 nominee for the Howard Hughes Medical Investigator Award she received honours and awards including the NSF Career Advancement Award, and the Medical Research Council of Canada Postdoctoral Fellowship. She is a recipient of the Presidential Award for Excellence in Science, Mathematics and Engineering Mentoring.

Roger Evon Hunter (Dr.) – Neurosurgeon, First Caribbean recipient of the prestigious Braakman Diploma and prize from The European Association of Neurosurgical Societies (EANS).

Rosemary Moodie (Dr) - Moodie is a Jamaican born physician and neonatologist/newborn intensive care specialist at Canada's top children's hospital She's also an associate professor of paediatrics at the University of Toronto Medical School. In 2015 the Royal College of Physicians and Surgeons of Canada awarded Moodie the Prix d'excellence – Specialist of the Year award. In the same year, she was awarded RBC's Top 25 Canadian Immigrant Award. In 2014 the city of Toronto awarded Moodie the prestigious Constance E Hamilton Award on the Status of Women, for "securing equitable treatment for women". She was appointed to the Canadian Senate in 2018.

Theresa Rambaran (Dr) - In 2018, she was awarded the prestigious Marie Sklodowska-Curie Seal of Excellence by the European Commission, and a year later received the Kempe Foundation Postdoctoral Fellowship. She is conducting research at the Department of Public Health and Clinical Medicine at Umeå University in Sweden which involves the use of clinical trials to guide the development of supplements from Nordic berries which are intended to counter cardiometabolic dysfunctions.

Thomas Phillip Lecky (Dr.) – Pioneered the scientific development of Jamaican livestock resulting in the first breed of indigenous cattle, Jamaica Hope, Jamaica Red, Jamaica Brahman and Jamaica Black cattle breeds.

William E. McCulloch (Dr.) - Found a cure for Black Water Fever and Trypanosomiasis (sleeping sickness).

Yvette Francis-McBarnette (Dr) – Jamaican born American pediatrician and a pioneer in treating children with sickle cell anaemia. In 1946, aged 19, she enrolled at the Yale School of Medicine - she was the second black woman at the school. Later in

1966, together with colleagues Dr. Doris Wethers and Dr. Lila Fenwick, she started the Foundation for Research and Education in Sickle Cell Disease.

SPORTS

Alia Atkinson – First black woman to win a world swimming title. Atkinson is the world record holder and one of only three women to ever to have broken the 29-second barrier in the 50 metres breaststroke. She is also currently tied with Ruta Meilutyte for the 100 metres breaststroke world record. Atkinson owns eight of the 14 sub-29 swims in history.

Allan 'Skill' Cole – Youngest player to represent Jamaica at the national level and first Jamaican footballer to play in the Brazilian first division when he signed with Nautico in 1971.

Arthur Wint – Won Jamaica's first Olympic gold medal for the 400 m and silver for the 800m.

Asafa Powell – Held the 100 m world record between June 2005 and May 2008. He has the most sub-10 second times over 100 m.

Bertland Cameron – First Jamaican to win the gold in an individual event at the first World Championships held in Helsinki, Finland.

Bunny Grant – Former Commonwealth lightweight boxing champion.

Charles Theodore 'Chili' Davis – Jamaican born former outfielder/designated hitter who played in Major League Baseball with the San Francisco Giants (1981-87), California Angels (1988-90, 1993-96), Minnesota Twins (1991-92), Kansas City Royals (1997) and New York Yankees (1998-99).

Charmaine Crooks – Jamaica born Canadian athlete is a five-time Olympian and Olympic Silver Medallist. She represented Canada for close to 20 years in Athletics. The first Canadian woman to run 800 meters in under two minutes, she won Gold medals at the Pan American, Commonwealth, World Cup, and the World Student Games.

Connie Francis – Played in five World Netball Champion-ships between 1986 and 2003 and helped lift Jamaica's world ranking from fifth to third during that period.

Part III: Symbols, People, Places and Things

Courtney Walsh – Former captain of the West Indies Cricket team and world record holder for most test wickets between 2000 and 2004.

Daniel Thomas-Dodd - Jamaica's first ever medallist in the women's shot put event at the Olympic or World Championships level. She also is the first Caribbean woman to medal in the event at the World Championships.

David Weller – Track cyclist who won a bronze medal in the 1000 m time trial at the **1980 Summer Olympics in Moscow,** becoming the first Jamaican to win an Olympic medal in another sport other than track and field.

Deon Hemmings – First ever Jamaican woman to win an Olympic Gold in the 400m hurdles

Donald Quarrie – One of the few athletes who have held the 100m and 200m world records simultaneously. He won gold and silver medals at the 1976 Montreal Olympics.

Donovan Bailey – Jamaican born sprinter who represented Canada and once held the world record for the **100 metre** race following his gold medal performance in the **1996 Olympic Games.** He was the first Canadian to legally break the **10-second barrier** in the 100 m.

Elaine Thompson – Became double Olympic champion by winning the women's 100 metres and 200 metres at the 2016 Rio Olympics.

Federick Dacres – First Jamaican to win a global senior medal in the discus, a silver at the World Championships in Doha.

George Headley - Universally acknowledged as one of the finest batsmen of all time with batting average of 60.83 in test cricket

George Rhoden – First West Indian to win two gold medals at the same Olympics.

Grace Jackson – Won Olympic silver medal in Seoul behind Florence Griffiths Joyner, the fastest woman in Olympic history.

Herb McKinley – the only person in history to have won Olympic medals in both the 100 and 400 metres and the only person to reach the 100, 200 and 400 metres finals.

James Beckford – World Championship and Olympic silver medalist in the long jump.

Jeff Cunningham – **Jamaican**-born **American** Major League Soccer player.

Jeffrey Dujon - West Indies wicketkeeper/batsman scalped 272 victims from 81 matches and scored over 3,332 runs with five centuries.

John Barnes – Jamaican-born English football manager and former player who was widely considered as one of the best wingers in the history of football. During his playing career, he had successful periods at Watford and Liverpool in the 1980s and 1990s, winning the First Division twice, the FA Cup twice, and playing for England 79 times, then a record for a black player.

Juliet Cuthbert – Won Olympic silver medal in the 100 and 200 metres.

Lascelles Brown – **Jamaican**-born **Canadian bobsledder** who has competed since 1999 (**Canada** since 2004). Competing in three **Winter Olympics**, he is the first Jamaican-born athlete to win a Winter Olympic medal.

Lawrence Rowe – First batsman to score centuries in both innings on his test debut.

Leon Bailey - Jamaican professional footballer who plays as a winger for Bundesliga club Bayer Leverkusen

Lindy Delapenha – First Jamaican to play professional football in England. He won a league championship medal with Portsmouth and was leading scorer for Middlesbrough in the 1951-52, 1953-54 and 1955-56 seasons.

Linford Christie – Jamaican born sprinter who specialised in the 100 metres. He is the only British man to win a gold medal in the 100 m at all four major competitions: the Olympic Games and the World, Commonwealth, and European championships. He was the first European to break the 10-second barrier in the 100 m.

Lloyd Honeyghan – Jamaican born WBC/WBA & IBF welterweight champion from 1986 to 1987 and WBC welterweight champion from 1988 to 1989.

Lorraine Fenton – Won a silver medal at the Sydney Olympics becoming the first Jamaican woman to medal in the event. She also won three individual world championship medals namely two silver and a bronze.

Maurice Smith – World Championship silver medallist in the decathlon.

Melaine Walker – World and Olympic 400 m hurdles champion. Her time of 52.42 seconds at the 2009 World Championships in **Berlin** is the second fastest time in history.

Merlene Ottey – Most women's World Championships medals (fourteen) and most Olympic appearances (seven).

Michael Holding – One of the most charismatic and feared fast-bowlers in the all-conquering West Indies sides of the 1970s and 1980s. Often remembered for what is often described as "the greatest over in Test history", which he bowled in 1981 in **Bridgetown** to English batsman Geoff Boycott. He is now a distinguished analyst of cricket in print and on TV.

Mike McCallum – Held world titles in several weight classes in boxing.

Omar McLeod – First Jamaican man to hold 110m World and Olympic titles simultaneously .

Patrick A. Ewing – Jamaican born eleven time NBA All-Star; One of 50 Greatest Players in NBA History and Two-time Olympic gold medalist (1984, '92) competing for the USA.

Percy Hayles – Former Commonwealth lightweight boxing champion.

Raheem Sterling – is a Jamaican born English professional footballer who plays as a winger and attacking midfielder.

Raymond Stewart – The first man to appear in three Olympic 100 metre finals.

Ricardo Fuller – Footballer who played for Stoke City in the British Premier League.

Ricardo Gardner – Footballer who played for Bolton wanderers in the British Premier League.

Robin Fraser – Jamaican born American Soccer player who played six seasons in the **American Professional Soccer League** and ten seasons in Major League Soccer. He earned 27 caps with the United States men's national soccer team between 1988 and 2001.

Samardo Samuels – Jamaican born power forward/centre for the University of Louisville Cardinals men's basketball team. He was named the 2008 USA today high school player of the year and was a McDonald's All-American. Samuels was the number one ranked power forward in his high school class by Scout.com and was ranked number two by Rivals.com.

Sanya Richards – Jamaican born sprinter who competes for the USA. She has won two Olympic gold medals in the 4 x 400 metres relay and a World Championship individual gold medal in the 400 metres.

Shelly Ann Fraser – Double Olympic gold medallist and four times World champion. First woman to hold both titles simultaneously and widely regarded as the best female sprinter ever.

Tajay Gayle – Became the first Jamaican man to win gold in the long jump at the World Championship in Doha.

Tessa Sanderson – British javelin thrower who still remains the only female athlete to win an Olympic gold throwing medal for Great Britain which she accomplished in 1984. She competed in six Olympic Games and also won many other major medals including three Commonwealth Gold medals.

Trecia Smith – World Championship gold medallist in the triple jump.

Usain Bolt - First man to set world records in three sprinting events at a single Olympics and first man to hold the 100 m and 200 m World and Olympic titles simultaneously.

Veronica Campbell-Brown – Five time Olympic medallist and the second woman in history to win two consecutive Olympic 200 m events.

Yohan Blake – Became the youngest ever world champion in the 100m when he won gold at the 2011 World Championships in Daegu.

Combined Martial Arts Team - Jamaica amassed 68 medals — 21 gold, 20 silver, and 27 bronze medals at the International Sports Karate Association United States Open in July 2017. In 2018 Jamaica's Mixed Martial Arts team had their best ever showing at the International Sport Karate and Kickboxing

Amateur World Championships in Montego Bay Conference Centre, winning 27 gold, 34 silver and 56 bronze medals.

Bobsled Team – This was the first Caribbean bobsled team to qualify for the winter sport. The feat led to the production of the Hollywood movie "Cool Runnings".

Netball Team – Jamaica has played in every world championship. They have finished in third place on three occasions the last time in 2007 in Auckland, New Zealand. In 2018 the senior team was ranked number one in the Caribbean and third in the world behind Australia and New Zealand.

Reggae Girlz – In 2018 became the first Caribbean team to qualify for a women's football World Cup in France. Their qualification comes on the 20th anniversary of the men's team reaching their first World Cup, in 1998 - also held in France.

Reggae Boyz – The 1998 national football team created history by becoming the first English-speaking Caribbean team to reach World Cup.

Other Outstanding Jamaicans

Alvin Curling - Curling, migrated to Canada in 1967 and became the first Black Canadian to hold a Cabinet position in Ontario and later the first Black Speaker of the Ontario Legislature. In 2014 he received the Order of Ontario which is the province's highest official honour.

Angela King – Was a Jamaican Diplomat who for decades served at the United Nations in several senior positions. She was a special adviser to former United Nations Secretary-General, Kofi Annan on gender issues and the advancement of women. She also chaired the UN's inter-agency network on women and gender equality and oversaw the activities of the Department for the Advancement of Women for which she had previously been the director. Between 1992 and 1994 she was chief of mission of the U.N. Observer Mission to South Africa.

Angella Reid – First Female to be appointed White House Chief Usher during the Obama administration. Her formal title will be director of the president's executive residence and chief usher. She will be responsible for executive residence activities, as well as operations on the executive residence grounds.

Barbara Gloudon – OD, OJ, Journalist, author, playwright, talk show host, lecturer and cultural activist dedicated to preserving the cultural authenticity of Jamaican theatre. She wrote several of Jamaica's Pantomimes. When she isn't tackling social and cultural issues on radio, she lectures locally and internationally on themes of Caribbean cultural/socio-economic identity. In addition to the Order of Distinction and Order of Jamaica she has received a number of awards including Seprod Gold Medals for excellence in journalism, Bronze Musgrave Medal and the Centenary Medal in recognition of cultural contribution.

Barrington Irving – Youngest person to pilot a plane **around the world solo.** He is also the first black person and first Jamaican to accomplish this feat.

Beverly Hall – Was one of the foremost educators in the United States. When she became the 15th appointed superintendent of the Atlanta Public Schools (APS) in 1999, she promised to transform the district into a world-class school system, using nationally proven reform models, facility upgrades and business operations redesign. Under her leadership, standardized test scores have risen, aging facilities have been renovated and a new blueprint for business operations is being implemented. She was named the 2009 National Superintendent of the Year.

Carmen Stewart – Known for her religious contribution, she started the Wilbert Stewart Basic School in 1976. In partnership with the HEART Trust NTA, she established the Pentecostal Gospel Temple skills training project and along with her husband formed the Pentecostal Gospel Temple in the 1960s. In 1996, she served as deputy governor general, the first woman to do so. She was awarded the Order of Distinction for Health Education and Religion in 1986 and was the recipient of the Prime Minister's Jamaica 21 Award in the field of religion.

Carolyn Gomes O.J. – Human rights activist, Dr. Gomes is the co-founder of Jamaicans for Justice. On December 10, 2008, Dr. Gomes received the prestigious United Nations Prize in the Field of Human Rights.

Claude Chin – As the coach of Jamaica's combined martial arts team he guided them to a 35-match win streak for the last six years, including three International **Sports** Karate Association US Open World Continental Team Fighting championships. He has also guided the likes of Nicholas Dussard, Kenneth Edwards and

Alrick Wanliss to world titles at the US Open and the International Tae kwon do Federation's (ITF) World Cup.

Douglas Orane – He served as the Chief Executive Officer of Grace Kennedy Limited from 1995 to 2011 and also served as its Chairman from 1998 to 2012. Orane served as President of the Private Sector Organisation of Jamaica from 1992 to 1994 and as its Vice President from 2001 to 2003. He was an Independent Senator in the Senate from 1998 to 2002. He also served as the Chairman of First Global Bank Limited until September 19, 2017.

Elaine Bryan – Atlanta-based Jamaican multi-award winning high school counsellor, realtor, empowerment speaker and financial columnist. She was awarded the 2008 DeKalb County Counsellor of the year in Atlanta, Georgia. In 2008 she was accepted into the prestigious Leadership Sandy Springs, a nexus for all sectors of the community. Her other awards include: Judge Glenda Hatchett Educational Mentoring Award; Turner Broadcasting Systems Award for Educational Excellence and Mayor Shirley Franklin Phoenix Award for Outstanding Achievement in Education. She is also featured on one of the stamps of the state of Georgia.

Eric Irons – Served in the in the Royal Air Force during World War Two and became Britain's first black magistrate in 1962.

Gordon Gill - Gordon Gill is an architect and one of the world's preeminent exponents of performance-based design. A founding partner of award-winning Adrian Smith + Gordon Gill Architecture, Gordon's work includes the design of the world's first net zero-energy skyscraper, the Pearl River Tower (designed at SOM Chicago), the world's first large-scale positive energy building, Masdar Headquarters. Prior to founding AS+GG in 2006, Gordon was an Associate Partner at Skidmore, Owings & Merrill which designed the world's then tallest building, Jeddah Tower in Saudi Arabia.

Ian Boyne – Was a journalist, talk show host, TV presenter and communications executive who won a number of journalism awards, both in Print and in Television and is the only Jamaican journalist with shows on radio, television and a column in print. He is host of the longest-running non-seasonal programme on Jamaican television 'Profile', the number one programme on television in its slot and authors the most read Gleaner column. His interviewing skills have seen him appearing on the front pages of the Washington Post and generated interest from other international media houses.

Jenna Wolfe –American journalist and personal trainer. She was a correspondent for NBC's Today, Sunday co-anchor and news anchor for Weekend Today. In 2014 Wolfe left the weekend Today show for a new role as lifestyle and fitness correspondent on the weekday Today show and NBC News.

Jody-Anne Maxwell – Winner of the 1998 Scripps National Spelling Bee at the age of twelve. She was the first contestant from outside the United States and the first black student to win in the history of the competition.

Joel Sadler – Creator of the Jiapur Knee, a low-cost, high-performance artificial knee for the developing world which is helping amputees especially in India to walk again.

Keith Valentine Graham (Levi Roots) – Musician, chef and entrepreneur. He was nominated for a MOBO award in 1998 and gained widespread fame after appearing on the UK television programme Dragons' Den looking for funding for his "Reggae Reggae Sauce". The sauce range continues to grow with Caribbean inspired cooking sauces, ketchup, dipping sauces, pasties. He has appeared in a television series 'Caribbean Cooking Made Easy.

Ken Ramsay – A noted photographer whose work is known in Europe and the United States. He is the author of 'Dare to Dream and the "The Dream lives on" - a Retrospect of Black and White Photographs'.

Kenneth Edwards – A teacher of Chinese Martial Arts in Pasadena, California, Kenneth Edwards also appeared in the 1995 film adaptation of the hit fighting video game Mortal Kombat. He's trained in many styles of martial arts, including Northern Praying Mantis and Tam Toi Moon. He's also an active member of the Ying Jow Pai International Kung Fu Association.

Kevin Fenton (Professor) – Expert in public health medicine, infectious disease epidemiology, HIV prevention and sexual health. He has worked in research, policy development and programme leadership at the global, national and local levels. Although born in Scotland he grew up and was educated in Jamaica at both the secondary and tertiary levels. In 2017 he was announced as Southwark Council's new Director of Health and Wellbeing working on secondment from Public Health England.

Lord Bill Morris OJ – Former General Secretary of the Transport and General Workers Union and the first black leader of a major British trade union. His interests have spanned directorships of the Bank of England and the England and Wales Cricket Board. He was knighted in 2003 and was awarded a life peerage. He took his seat in the House of Lords in June 2006 and took the title: Lord Morris of Handsworth.

Lorna Lewis - The first woman of color to preside over the New York State Council of School Superintendents, which represents more than 800 top education leaders statewide.

Lucille Mathurin Mair – Was a Jamaican ambassador, author, diplomat and gender specialist. She served as Assistant Secretary-General in the office of the United Nations Secretary in 1979, from which she performed the role of Secretary-General for the World Conference of the United Nations Decade for Women held in 1980 in Copenhagen. From 1981- 1982, she served as special advisor to the United Nations Children's Fund (UNICEF) on Women's Development at the level of assistant secretary general. She then went on to serve as Secretary-General of the United Nations Conference on Palestine from 1982 to 1987.

Margarett Best – Jamaican born Canadian and former politician elected to the Legislative Assembly of Ontario in the 2007 provincial election, representing the riding of Scarborough—Guildwood. She was appointed the Minister of Health Promotion after the 2007 election.

Mary Seacole – Was a Healer, Nurse and great humanitarian, she risked everything and self financed her trip to Crimea in the mid 1850's to treat many soldiers were dying not from war wounds but from illnesses such as cholera and dysentery. She was also at the forefront in the fight against cholera and yellow fever both at home and abroad and as a result numerous foundations, research centres and associations are named in her honour.

Newton Marshall – The first Jamaican and the first black man to take part in the Yukon Quest dog race, a gruelling 1000 mile dogsled race across the Arctic tundra in Alaska. In the toughest dog race in the world, Newton crossed the Finish Line on the 26th February 2009 placing 13th out of 29 starters.

Patricia Durrant – First UN Ombudsman; among other honours, she is the recipient of the Distinguished Achievement Award from the World Association of Former United Nations Interns and Fellows.

Paulette Davy – based at the National Aeronautics and Space Administration Marshall Space Flight Centre in Huntsville, Alabama she won the Women's Equality Day award for outstanding administrative service in 2007. The award recognizes outstanding federal employees in professional, administrative and supervisory capacities. She also received several NASA awards, including the NASA Group Achievement award which recognizes employees for meeting and exceeding NASA's values and expectations, and the Sustained Superior Performance award which honours high-level performance of duties and responsibilities of the employee's assigned position, as evidenced by their current rating of record.

Philip Sherlock– Was a Caribbean scholar and educationist, best known for his long and dedicated service as a member of the University of the West Indies community. He was the founding principal of the new campus at St. Augustine, Trinidad, and undertook the establishment of the Faculty of Engineering as well as transformed and incorporated the Imperial College of Tropical Agriculture into that Campus. Sir Philip was internationally recognized as a leading Caribbean scholar, lecturer and author.

Ray Chen – World renowned photographer who has used his vast skills to tell pictorial stories that portray Jamaican life. It is through this medium that many have gained their first impressions that have so persuasively captured the essence and beauty of Jamaican life and places.

Richard Ho Lung – Founder and superior general of the Catholic charity Missionaries of the Poor. The work of the Missionaries of the Poor has attracted international attention, including visits by Mother Teresa in 1986; Francis Cardinal Arinze of Nigeria, and His Holiness Pope John Paul II in 1993. Father Ho Lung writes and composes music and also dedicates his life to spreading the message of the gospel through music. Each year, 'Father Ho Lung and Friends' stage a musical performance to raise funds to support the work of the Missionaries of the Poor. He has received numerous national and international awards and recognition for his contribution to music, humanitarian cooperation, and community service.

Ronald Alexander Blackwood - Jamaican-born American politician who served as the Mayor of Mount Vernon, New York. In 1985, Blackwood became the first black Mayor of Mount Vernon, as well as the first black person elected mayor of any municipality in New York State.

Rosemary Brown – Jamaican born Canadian politician who served as a Member of the Legislative Assembly (MLA) in the British Columbia legislature from 1972 to 1986, making her the first Black Canadian woman to be elected to a Canadian provincial legislature.

Saleem Josephs – Rewrote the history book on academic excellence at the prestigious Columbia University in New York City, becoming the first student from that institution to graduate with three degrees in one sitting. He was presented with the Doctor of Dental Surgery (DDS) degree and also received graduate degrees in Business Administration (MBA) and Public Health (MPA) from the prestigious Ivy League university. In addition to his three degrees, Josephs topped the 84-member graduating class of 2006 in the areas of community health and prosthodontics and was cited by the National Dental Honour Society, Omicron Kappa Upsilon, for outstanding scholarship.

Steve Bucknor – For many years regarded as one of the world's best cricket umpire. He stood in a world record 119 Test matches and officiated in an unprecedented fifth consecutive World Cup final match when Australia beat Sri Lanka in 2007. He was also a football referee with FIFA status.

Vincent "Randy" Chin – Record Producer and label owner who ran the Randy's shop, recording studio, and record label, later moving to New York City and setting up the VP Records empire, which became the world's largest independent label and distributor of Caribbean music in the world.

People of Jamaican Ancestry

Andrea Levy – widely regarded as the first black British author to achieve both critical and mainstream commercial success. Her novel Small Island won the Whitbread prize, the orange prize for fiction and the Commonwealth Writers' prize.

Ainsley Harriott – Celebrity chef, TV presenter and author. In 2000, he made his debut on US television in New York City. He has also appeared in television adverts.

Albert Lincoln Roker Jr. - American weather forecaster, journalist, television personality, actor and author. He is also CEO of Al Roker Entertainment a leading producer of original, award-winning TV programs and digital content for the world's best networks and brands.. He is the current weather anchor on NBC's Today. Roker also appears occasionally as a co-anchor on NBC Nightly News.

Alesha Dixon – British singer-songwriter, rapper, dancer, model television personality and judge on a number of reality shows. She first found fame in the all-female R&B/garage trio Mis-Teeq. In 2007 Dixon became a contestant on Strictly Come Dancing and eventually won.

Alexandra Burke – English singer and winner of the fifth series of UK television singing talent show The X Factor. Her prize, as winner, was a recording contract with Simon Cowell's Syco record label, whose parent company is Sony Music. In 2009 she became the first British female solo artist to sell a million copies of a single in the UK.

Alicia Augello Cook (Alicia Keys) – American recording artist, musician and actress. She became the best-selling new artist and best-selling R&B artist of 2001. Her album earned her five Grammy Awards in 2002 and her second studio album won her four more Grammy Awards in 2005.

Anthony G. Brown – Elected as Maryland's eighth Lieutenant Governor in 2006.

Ashley Simon Young – English footballer and world cup representative who played for Aston Villa and now at Manchester United.

Benjamin Zephaniah – UK born British Jamaican Rastafarian writer and dub poet. He spent his early years in Jamaica where he absorbed much of the music and poetry that influences his work. In 1989 he was nominated for Oxford Professor of Poetry, narrowly beaten by Seamus Heaney. He has also written two novels for teenagers, Face (1999), which was short-listed for the Children's Book Award in 2000, and Refugee Boy (2001).

Part III: Symbols, People, Places and Things

Beverley Knight – British soul and R&B singer, songwriter, and record producer who released her debut album in 1995. Widely labelled as one of Britain's greatest soul singers, she has one platinum and 4 gold albums as well as 3 MOBO awards.

Carl Winston Lumbly – American film, stage, and television actor known for the role of Marcus Dixon in the television drama Alias, and for the role of Martian Manhunter in the animated series Justice League and Justice League Unlimited. His first major role was Detective Marcus Petrie on the television series Cagney and Lacey (1982 – 1988). In 1987, he obtained positive reviews for his portrayal of Black Panther Party co-founder Bobby Seale in the HBO television movie Conspiracy.

Colin Ray Jackson – British sprint hurdling athlete and television commentator. Between 1993 and 2006 he held the world record in the 110 metre hurdles. He won the silver medal at the 1988 Summer Olympics and gold medals at two World Championships. He also won four consecutive European Championship gold medals from 1990 to 2002.

Colin Powell – Former United States Secretary of State (2001-2005) and Chairman of the Joint Chiefs of Staff (1989–1993).

Corbin Bleu Reivers – American actor, model, rapper, and singer known for his roles in the High School Musical film series, the Discovery Kids television series *Flight 29 Down,* and the Disney Channel Original Movie *Jump In!* in 2007.

Denise Lewis – British athlete and television commentator who specialised in the heptathlon. She won the gold medal in the heptathlon at the 2000 Sydney Olympics.

Diane Abbott – British Labour politician who has been the Member of Parliament for Hackney North and Stoke Newington. In 1987 she made history by becoming the first black woman ever elected to the British Parliament. She has since built a distinguished career as a parliamentarian, broadcaster and commentator.

Dina Asher-Smith – In 2019 became the first British woman to win a major global sprint title when she won the 200m in Doha

Franklin Roy Bruno – British boxer whose career highlight was winning the WBC Heavyweight championship in 1995. Altogether, he won 40 of his 45 contests. Frank is also an accomplished actor and he was awarded an MBE in 1990.

Gloria Reuben – Canadian singer and actress of film and television, known for her role as Jeanie Boulet on the popular hit medical drama ER and for her role of Rosalind Whitman in the TV show Raising the Bar.

Harold George "Harry" Belafonte Jr – American musician, actor and social activist. One of the most successful popular singers in history, he has been an advocate for civil rights and humanitarian causes.

Jade Ewen – British singer, songwriter, actress and member of the Sugababes since 2009. She represented the UK at the 2009 Eurovision Song Contest performing the Andrew Lloyd-Webber penned "It's My Time". She achieved fifth place, cementing her as the most successful British Eurovision act since 2002.

Jamelia Davis (Jamelia) – British singer-songwriter and model, most famous for her use of a capella and prolific work in the R&B genre. Three of her albums have reached the Top 40 and she has amassed eight UK top ten singles. In addition he has won four MOBO Awards, a Q Award and has received nine BRIT Award nominations.

Kamala Devi Harris – United States Senator from California and former District Attorney of San Francisco. She was cited by the New York Times to be among the most likely women to become the first female President of the United States. Following the election of Joe Biden as U.S. president in the 2020 election, Harris assumed office as vice president of the United States on January 20, 2021.

Kelly Holmes – British middle distance athlete. She won gold medals in the 800 metres and the 1,500 metres at the 2004 Summer Olympics and has World and European Championship medals. In 2005 she was honoured with Damehood by the Queen and won the Laureus World Sports Woman of the Year Award.

Kerry Marisa Washington - American actress. Since 2012, Washington has gained wide public recognition for starring in the ABC drama Scandal. She has been nominated twice for a Primetime Emmy Award for Outstanding Lead Actress in a Drama Series, Screen Actors Guild Award for Outstanding Performance by a Female Actor in a Drama Series, and a Golden Globe Award for Best Actress in a Television Series.

Kreesha Turner – Canadian R&B/Pop Recording artist. Her third single, "Don't Call Me Baby", became her first Canadian Top 10 single.

Laban Roomes – Founder of Goldgenie - a specialist gift and gold plating company. He achieved fame when he was invited to the Emmys in Hollywood to present Gold plated phones to the likes of Denzel Washington and then when he appeared on the BBC TV series Dragon's Den and won investment from Dragon Jams Caan. He has helped many people set up & run their own successful plating businesses.

Lincoln MacCauley Alexander - First elected black official in the Canadian parliament. He served as the 24th Lieutenant Governor of Ontario from 1985 to 1991. Alexander was also a Governor of the Canadian Unity Council.

Lee Jasper – Leading expert on police and black community relationships in the UK. He became known as the UK's most prominent race relations activist and adviser, sitting on many different committees and groups and founded a range of national black organisations.

Lennox Lewis – Retired boxer and former undisputed World heavyweight champion. He won gold for Canada at the 1988 Olympic Games as an amateur. Lewis is one of only five boxers in history to have won the heavyweight championship three times. Throughout his professional career he suffered only two losses, both of which he avenged in rematches.

Lenworth George Henry – Sir Henry is or has been an actor, writer, comedian, television presenter and University Chancellor. One of the founders of comic relief a key member of their fundraising team he won a Royal Television Society Silver Award medal for outstanding contributions to multi-ethnic programming in the UK, through his production company Crucial Films. He was knighted in 2015.

Lester Holt Jr. - American journalist and news anchor for the weekday edition of NBC Nightly News and Dateline NBC. He is the first African-American to solo anchor a weekday network nightly newscast.

Louis Farrakhan (born Louis Eugene Walcott) – National Representative of the Nation of Islam. He is an advocate for black interests, and a critic of American society.

Marsha Lisa Thomason - English television and film actress who is best known for playing Nessa Holt in the first two seasons of the NBC series Las Vegas, Naomi Dorrit on the ABC series Lost, and FBI agent Diana Berrigan on the USA Network series White Collar.

Mike Fuller – Britain's first black Chief Constable. He was the founding chair of the Black Police Association and was responsible for setting up Operation Trident, the unit set up to tackle black on black crime within London urban communities.

Mýa Marie Harrison - American **R&B** singer-songwriter, record producer, actress, and model whose eponymous debut album with **Interscope Records** was released in April 1998 and sold over two million copies in the USA In 2001, Mýa joined with Lil Kim, Pink and Christina Aguilera for a remake of "Lady Marmalade," which won each a grammy award.

Naomi Campbell – **British** supermodel who started her career in the 1980s and soon appeared on the catwalks of Milan and Paris as well as on the cover pages of internationally renowned fashion magazines. She is also known for perfumes associated with her name.

Niomi Arleen McLean-Daley (Ms Dynamite) – British R&B, UK garage, hip hop singer and rapper. She is a double BRIT Award winner along with three MOBO awards. In 2002, she won the prestigious Mercury Music Prize.

Peter Sloly – The youngest Deputy Chief ever in the Toronto police force and only the second black person in the history of the Toronto Police Service (TPS) to be made its Deputy Chief. In 2001 he was part of the United Nations Peacekeeping Mission to Kosovo and was a Command Staff Officer and the Canadian Contingent Commander.

Samantha Majendie-Albert – Canadian-born equestrian who represents Jamaica in international competition.

Shane West – American actor, musician and songwriter. He has appeared in the television series ER and Once and Again and the film A Walk to Remember.

Sheryl Lee Ralph – American **actress** and singer who in 1973 was crowned Miss Black Teen-age New York. At 19, she was the youngest female to ever graduate from Rutgers University. She has appeared in films such as The Mighty Quinn, Mistress, The

Flintstones, Deterrence and Unconditional Love. On television, she is known for playing Etienne Toussaint-Bouvier on Designing Women and later Dee Mitchell on Moesha.

Sheila Jackson Lee - She is currently the United States Representative for Texas's 18th congressional district, currently serving in her 13th term in the House, having served since 1995. She is a member of the Judicial and Homeland Committees.

Shirley Thompson – Award-winning composer having written numerous scores for opera, contemporary dance, orchestra, film and television. She is the first British woman to have composed and conducted a symphony for 30 years and the first black woman ever to do so. She was also the first black woman to compose music for the British Broadcasting Corporation (BBC) In 1995, she established her own chamber orchestra - The Shirley Thompson Ensemble where she developed her style of fusing classical orchestrations with popular dance and vocals. 1998 saw her directing her first film, Memories in Mind (BBC2) and in 2001 she performed for HM the Queen at Westminster Abbey.

Susan Elizabeth Rice - American public official who served on President Barack Obama's Cabinet as the U.S. ambassador to the United Nations and was the 24th United States National Security Advisor from 2013 to 2017. A Rhodes Scholar, while at Oxford Rice won the Chatham House-British International Studies Association Prize for the most distinguished doctoral dissertation in the United Kingdom in the field of International Relations.

Tarrus Riley - Reggae singer and son of veteran reggae singer Jimmy Riley. Riley has consistently racked up awards for his work. Among his accolades are Best Singer, Male Vocalist, Cultural Artiste, Song of the Year and Best Song. Some of the awards institutions which have rewarded Riley include the Youth View Awards, The Star People's Choice Awards, EME Awards, and the Reggae Academy award.

Theo Walcot – English footballer who plays as a winger for Arsenal and the English National Team.

Tonya Lee Williams – Canadian actress, best known for her role as Dr. Olivia Barber Winters on the American **soap opera** The Young and the Restless, from 1990 to 2005, and for a brief time in 2007.

Tyson Beckford – American model and actor best known as a Ralph Lauren Polo model. He was also the host of both seasons of the Bravo program Make Me a Supermodel. Beckford has often been described as the most successful male supermodel of all time.

Wentworth Earl Miller III – English-born, American actor who rose to stardom following his role as Michael Scofield in the Fox Network television series Prison Break.

Yvette Diane Clarke – Member of the United States House of Representatives from New York's 11th congressional district. She is the Chairwoman of the Subcommittee on Emerging Threats, Cybersecurity, Science and Technology.

Famous people who made Jamaica home

Chris Blackwell, President & CEO of Island Records and Palm Pictures, New York City. One of the first to record the Jamaican popular music that eventually became known as ska music. Blackwell is also credited with bringing Bob Marley & the Wailers to the attention of international audiences.

Noel Coward (1899-1973) British-born playwright, songwriter and actor. After numerous years of entertaining dignitaries such as Queen Elizabeth both on stage and at his Jamaican home, Coward was knighted in 1970. He died at his beloved Firefly in 1973 and is buried there, his grave overlooking Blue Harbour.

Ian Fleming (1908-1964) Writer of the most famous spy and action hero James Bond Fleming purchased land in Oracabessa that had once been a donkey racecourse and designed a house he called Goldeneye.

Errol Flynn (1909-1959) Famous for his roles as Captain Blood and Robin Hood. Flynn dubbed Port Antonio heaven on earth and made investments in a cattle farm and the Titchfield Hotel, which he hoped would help to stimulate tourism in Port Antonio.

Dignitaries & famous people who visited Jamaica post Independence (first 50 years)

1962 - Her Royal Highness Princess Margaret
1962 - Lyndon Johnson, Vice President, United States

Part III: Symbols, People, Places and Things

- 1965 - Dr. Martin Luther King, Civil Rights Leader, US National Hero
- 1966 - Mohammed Ali
- 1966 - 1986 Mother Teresa
- 1966 - 1983, 2002 HM Queen Elizabeth II and HRH Prince Philip
- 1966 - HRH Prince Charles and Princess Anne
- 1966 - His Imperial Majesty Haile Selassie I, Emperor of Ethiopia
- 1966 - President Kenneth Kaunda of Zambia
- 1971 - Edson Arantes Do Nascimento (Pele)
- 1971 - President Jose Figueres, Costa Rica
- 1973 - George Foreman & Joe Frazier (World Heavyweight Title Fight)
- 1974 - President Julius Nyerere of Tanzania
- 1975 - President Samora Moises Machel, Mozambique
- 1977 - 2000, 2005 President Fidel Castro, Cuba
- 1982 - President Ronald Reagan, United States of America
- 1982 - President Karl Carstens, Germany
- 1982 - President Louis Herrerra Campin, Venezuela
- 1986 - Archbishop Desmond Tutu, South Africa
- 1987 - Rt. Hon. Margaret Thatcher, Prime Minister of Britain
- 1987 - President Miguel de la Madrid, Mexico
- 1987 - President Dr. Auelt Masire, Botswana
- 1991 - Mr. Nelson Mandela, Leader of the ANC, South Africa
- 1993 - Pope John Paul II
- 1994 – Gen. Colin Powell, 1st African American Sec. of State, USA
- 1995 - President Robert Mugabe, Zimbabwe
- 1997 - President Jerry Rawlings, Ghana
- 1998 - Kofi Annan, United Nations Secretary General
- 2000 - HRH Prince Phillip, England
- 2002 - President Olusegun Obasanjo, Nigeria
- 2002 - Louis Farrakhan, Leader of the Nation of Islam
- 2004 - President Thabo Mbeki, South Africa
- 2007 - President Luiz Inacio Lula da Silva, Brazil
- 2007 - Dr. John Sentamu, Archbishop of York
- 2009 - King Juan Carlos I and Queen Sophia
- 2009 - Vice President Xi Jinping, People's Republic of China
- 2009 - President Jakaya Mrisho Kikwete, United Republic of Tanzania
- 2010 - Hilary Clinton, Secretary of State, USA
- 2012 - HRH, Prince Harry of Wales

Food and Drink

Ackee and Saltfish
Fried plantains, callaloo, green bananas and Johnny cake (fried dumpling

Jamaican Curry Goat
Traditional dish that is filled with loads of flavour and spices.

Jamaican Patties
Savoury and spicy pastry filled meat or vegetables

Mackerel Run Down
Pickled mackerel, coconut milk, herbs and spices

Jerk Chicken

Escoveitch Fish

Part III: Symbols, People, Places and Things

Bammy

Oxtail

Sweet Potato Pudding

Blue Draws
(also called tie-a-leaf)

Cow Cod Soup

Mannish Water

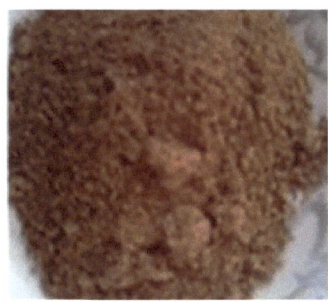
**Asham
(Parched Corn)**

Coffee
There are two main types of Jamaican coffee Blue Mountain and Prime. Blue Mountain must be grown in prescribed areas of the Blue Mountains. Jamaica Prime is grown in other areas.

Coconut Drops

Gizzada

Grater Cake

Sorrel
Drink made from the Sorrel Plant and is popular at Christmas

Jamaican Spice (Easter) Bun

Bulla Cake and Pear (Avocado)

Ginger Beer
One of the oldest and most known drink in several countries

Red Stripe Beer
A favourite in Jamaica and famous around the world for its great taste and refreshing qualities.

Jamaican Ting
Drink made from Grapefruit and is also used in combination with a variety of spirits.

Jamaican Rum
Jamaica produces a wide variety of rum (white, dark, spiced, aged, overproof, golden and vintage). The island can produce up to 50 million litres of rum annually to sell in over 70 countries.

Part III: Symbols, People, Places and Things

Flora and Fauna

Jamaica ranks 5th among the world's islands in terms of endemic life. There are 28 species of birds, 830 flowering plants, 82 ferns, 27 reptiles, 21 amphibians and 500 land snails found only in Jamaica.

Anthurium

Red Bougainvillea

Crotons

Hibiscus

White Orchid

Ginger Lilly

Heliconia

Joseph Coat

Bluebell

Annatto

Flamenco Dwarf

Poinciana

Jamaican Proverbs and Places and Symbols

Part III: Symbols, People, Places and Things

Zebra Butterfly
Jamaica has some 134 butterfly and moth species of which 20 are endemic.

Green Anole
One of the 7 species of Anolis on the island

Jamaican Iguana
One of the largest native land animals (endangered)

Tree Frog
Popular Jamaican animal often hiding in trees

Jamaican Coney
Terrestrial land mammal found in the rocky, forested areas of **Jamaica**

Jamaican Crocodile
Protected species usually found in mangroves, rivers and swamps

Jamaican Proverbs and Places and Symbols

Woodpecker
Jamaica's bird population contains about 280 species of which 30 are endemic and 19 sub-species are endemic.

Hawk or Chicken Hawk
A bird of prey that may also attack chickens hence the nickname

Rooster
Very popular in rural homes

Donkey
Beast of burden found in rural areas.

The Jamaican Doctor Bird
(Humming Bird)

Yellow Billed Parrot

Part III: Symbols, People, Places and Things

The Jamaican Owl
Also referred to as Patoo

Jamaican Swallowtail Butterfly (endangered)

Manatee
Large gentle creature often known locally as sea cows can weigh 1000 lbs and measure one to four meters in length.

The White-Tailed Deer (Odocoileus virginianus) is emerging as an alien invasive species

Jamaican Yellow Boa
(Epicrates Subflavus)
Jamaica is home to seven known species of snakes none of which are venomous. This is the largest snake species on the island, capable of growing up to 6 ½ feet.

Mongoose
The mongoose, a fearsome hunter is said to be responsible for decimating the ground bird population and some indigenous snakes and lizards.

Medicinal herbs grown in Jamaica

Jamaican Ball Moss
(Tillandsia recurvate)

Aloe Vera
(Sinkle bible)

Marijuana/Ganja

Arrow Root
Aloe Vera/Sinkle-Bible (*Aloe barbadensis*)
Ball Moss
Bissy
Bitterwood
Blood wisp
Cayenne pepper
Cerasse
Chainy Root/Wild yam root/China Root (*Smilax balbisiana*)
Cinnamon
Comfrey (*Symphytum officinale*)
CornSilk -The hair of the corn
Dandelion/Wild coffee (*Taraxacum officinale*)
Dog blood
Dogwood *(Piscidia erythrina/Piscidia piscipula)*
Duppy gun
Fresh Cut
Fever Grass (*Andropogon citrates/ Cymbopogon citrates*)
Garlic
Ginger
Ginkgo/Ginkgo biloba
Hog Head
Jack in a bush (*Eupatorium odoratum*)
+Leaf of life (*Bryophyllum pinnatum*)
Medina
Nettle/Stinging Nettle (*Urtica urens/Urtica dioica*)
Orange peel
Periwinkle/Ramgoat roses
Quassia chips
Red Clover
Samson/bee bush
Sarsaparilla *(Smilax ornate)*
Shame-a-Macca/ Shane O Lady
Siberian ginseng
Sorrel
Soursop (*Annona muricata*)
Spanish Needle
Spirit Weed
Stiff cock
Strong back
Vervine/love bush
Yohimbe

Jamaica's Parishes

Parish profiles together with places to visit and experiences to enjoy

Clarendon - Located at the southern side of Jamaica, roughly halfway between the eastern and western ends of the island. It is bordered on the north by St. Ann, on the west by Manchester, on the east by St. Catherine and on the south by the Caribbean Sea. The main towns are May Pen and Chapleton. Other important towns include Hayes, Frankfield, Rocky Point and Lionel Town.

- The curative waters of Milk River Bath
- Portland Point Lighthouse
- St Peter's Church and Moneymusk Library
- Jamaica's annual Agricultural Society's Farm Show at Denbigh
- Colbeck Castle Great House

Hanover - It lies to the west of St. James and to the north of Westmoreland. The capital, Lucea, is situated on a beautiful harbour 25 miles west of Montego Bay and midway between Montego Bay and Negril. The highest point is Birch Hill (1810 ft or 550.2 m), followed by Dolphin Head (1789 ft or 543.8 m). Numerous caves, coves and bays mark the coastline of Hanover. The main towns are Lucea, Green Island, Hopewell and Sandy Bay.

- Tryall Estate
- Hiking behind the hills of cousins cove
- Maryland Falls
- The Great Morass crocodile habit
- Bloody Bay
- Tryall Beach and Country Club

Kingston & St Andrew – Kingston the capital of Jamaica is located on the south-eastern end of the island. It is home to the world renowned places such as Kingston Harbour, the seventh largest harbour in the world also considered one of the finest anchorages and the Jamaica Conference Centre, an architectural masterpiece constructed in the late 1970s to house the International Law of the Sea Secretariat. St Andrew lies to the north, west and east of Kingston. St. Andrew stretches from Cross Roads to Rockfort in the east, and reaches up into the Blue Mountains, sharing borders with St. Thomas, Portland, St. Mary and St. Catherine.

- The Blue Mountains
- Devon House for gifts and ice cream
- Jamaica House
- Kings House
- The National Gallery
- Carnival after Easter
- Dining and partying in New Kingston
- Hope Gardens
- The Craft Market
- The St Andrew Parish Church, built in 1700.
- The Half-Way-Tree Clock and tower built in 1913 as a memorial to King Edward VII of England
- Snorkelling at Lime Cay (featured in the film "The Harder they Come")
- Port Royal
- The Bob Marley Museum
- Rockfort Mineral Bath
- Vale Royal

Manchester - Located in south-central Jamaica. To its east is the parish of Clarendon while St. Elizabeth lies to its west and Trelawny to its north. It rivals its neighbour Trelawny for the title of Jamaica's most mountainous parish. The three main ranges running throughout the parish are the Carpenters

Mountains, the May Day Mountains and the Don Figueroa Mountains. The high altitudes are responsible for its cool climate. For this reason Mandeville has been and continues to be a popular place of settlement for British expatriates. The main towns are Mandeville, Christiana, Porus and Mile Gully.

- Hiking and horseback riding
- An eco tour of the rainforest
- Bird watching at Marshall's Pen Great House
- Little Ochie
- Touring the High Mountain Coffee and Chocolate Factory at Williamsfield, the Pickapepper Sauce Factory at Shooters Hill and the Bammy Factory in Mandeville
- The gallery at Bloomfield Great House,

Portland - Located on the north east coat of Jamaica the parish is known for its natural beauty, stunning beaches, lush vegetation, multiple caves and rivers as well as the peak of the Blue Mountain range. It is usually very rainy as it lies in the direct path of the north east trade winds that usually bring rain. The main towns are Port Antonio, widely regarded as the cradle of the tourist industry and Buff Bay.

- The Morant Point Lighthouse
- The mysterious waters of Blue Lagoon
- Hiking
- Boston Beach, Long bay Beach, Winifred's Beach, San San Beach and Frenchman's Cove
- A taste of Jamaica at Boston Jerk
- Pelew Island
- Navy Island (formerly owned by Errol Flyn)
- Crystal springs
- Surfing and Sport Fishing
- Reach Falls
- Rafting on the Rio Grande

- Nanny Town
- The Nonsuch Caves
- Somerset Falls

St Ann - Situated on the north coast of the island, St. Ann is bounded on the east by the parish of St. Mary, and on the west by the parish of Trelawny. It shares its southern borders with the parishes of St. Catherine and Clarendon. The largest of all the parishes it is known as 'The Garden Parish' for its bauxite, agriculture and livestock production and especially its tourist attractions. Some 60 caves have been noted throughout the parish, of which the most famous is the Green Grotto. The main towns are St. Ann's Bay, Discovery Bay, Runaway Bay, Ocho Rios, Moneague and Brown's Town.

- Dolphin Cove
- The Craft Markets
- Climbing Dunn's River Falls
- Going snorkelling, windsurfing and diving
- Nine Mile, the birthplace and shrine of Robert (Bob) Nesta Marley
- Viewing the historical architecture of Harmony Hall
- Wassi Art and see the creation of extraordinary handmade pottery
- Going horseback riding
- New Hope Great House and the ruins of Minard Great House.
- Fern Gully – 3 Miles of foliage lined with hundreds of species of fern said to be the largest fern arboretum in the world
- "Noisy Water" River Cave and "Rat Bat Hole".
- Sampling the hearty treats of Faiths Pen
- Green Grotto Caves
- Ocho Rios Marine Park, Shaw Park Gardens and the Coyaba River Garden

Part III: Symbols, People, Places and Things

- Seville Heritage Park and Columbus Park Museum
- Chukka Cove Adventures
- Going White River Rafting
- Swimming with dolphins at Dolphin Cove
- Going glass-bottom kayaking on the Caribbean Sea
- Taking the Jamaica Bobsled ride
- Enjoying a Mystic Mountain escapade
- Marcus Garvey Statue in St. Ann's Bay
- The Ruins of Edinburgh Castle
- The Watt Town Zion Church spiritual schoolroom
- Going River Tubing at White River Valley Adventure

St. Catherine - Located on the south coast between the parishes of St. Andrew to the east, Clarendon to the west, and St. Ann and St. Mary to the north. St. Catherine is the second most populous and the most rapidly growing parish, with large manufacturing and agriculture industries. The main towns are Spanish Town, Linstead, Old Harbour and Portmore which became a municipality in 2003.

- The Bog Walk Gorge
- The Rio Cobre
- Enjoying fish and festival at Hellshire beach
- Seeing Two Sisters' Cave & Mountain River Cave
- Linstead Market and the Linstead Anglican Church
- Caymanas Park & Golf & Country Club
- Guardsman Serenity Park
- Rodney Memorial & St Jago de la Vega Cathedral, Spanish Town
- Portmore – Jamaica's third city
- The People's Museum of Craft & Technology & White Marl Taino Museum

- The Historic Emancipation Square

St. Elizabeth - This parish lies to the southwest end of Jamaica, bordered on the north by St. James and Trelawny, on the south by the Caribbean Sea, on the west by the parish of Westmoreland and on the east by Manchester. The northern and north-eastern sections of the parish are mountainous, while an extensive plain occupies the central and southern districts. When the Spanish were defeated in 1655, the slaves who did not manage to flee to Cuba, retreated to the impenetrable Cockpit Country, which included parts of St. Elizabeth. These fleeing slaves became known the Maroons and, today, St. Elizabeth remains home to the Maroons of Accompong, one of the most famous Maroon towns in Jamaica. St. Elizabeth has several towns of importance. These are Black River, Santa Cruz, Malvern, Junction and Balaclava. Other organised towns within the parish are Maggoty, Lacovia, Bull Savanna, Southfield, Newell, New Market, Siloah and Middle Quarters.

- Taking a boat ride up the Black River
- Treasure Beach
- Tiers of cascading water at YS Falls
- Taking a tour through the HQ of Jamaica's Appleton rum
- Going Bird Watching
- Alligator Pond and alligator hole
- Taking in the view of Pedro Bluff, Cutlass Bay and Lovers Leap
- Enjoying a taste of mouth-watering seafood at Little Ochie
- Driving through Bamboo Ave - nature's perfect archway
- Taking a Black River Heritage Walking Tour

St. James - Positioned on the north-west end of Jamaica, St. James is a suburban parish bounded by Trelawny to the east, St. Elizabeth to the south and Hanover and Westmoreland to the west. Stretching from St. Elizabeth, the Nassau Mountains extend diagonally across St. James, ending in hills at a point south of Montego Bay. The main towns are Montego Bay (Jamaica's second city), Cambridge, Catadupa, Ipswitch, Anchovy and Montpelier.

- Rose Hall Great House
- Playing Golf
- Exploring the hidden caves, trails and waterfalls in the Cockpit Country
- Wining and dining at the Hip Strip
- Enjoying Reggae Sumfest in summer
- The sun-splashed shores of Doctors Cave Beach
- Going cliff diving
- Having a great night out and listening to Live Music

St. Mary - The parish is bordered by Portland in the East, St. Ann in the West, and parts of St. Catherine and St. Andrew in the South. It is mostly mountainous, rising up to almost 4000 feet at the highest point with just under thirteen per cent of its area having slopes below ten degrees. There are three main rivers in St. Mary: the Rio Nuevo River, Wag Water and White Rivers. The main towns are Port Maria and Oracabessa.

- Goldeneye where Ian Flemming created James Bond
- Touring Firefly museum - former home of Noel Coward artist, actor and playwright
- The Rio Nuevo, White River and the Wag Water river
- Castleton Botanical Gardens

St. Thomas - The parish is bordered by St. Andrew on the west, Portland on the north and the Caribbean Sea to the south. The land mass of St. Thomas ranges from the peaks of the Blue Mountains and John Crow Mountains down to sea-level. Subsidiary ridges of the Blue Mountain range, running from east to west across the island, come to their eastern end in St. Thomas. These include the Port Royal Mountain Range, which rises in some parts to 1,219.2m (4,000 feet) and stretches from above New Castle, in St. Andrew, to a point near the sea in the

Albion area of St. Thomas. The main towns are Morant Bay, Bath and Yallahs.

- The springs at Bath; visit bull bay and Cane River Falls
- Zion Hill, a site populated by Bobo Shanty Rastafarians
- The Queensbury Ridge monument to "Three-Finger" Jack Mansong, an eighteenth century "Robin Hood" character
- Sun Coast Adventure Park
- Bath Botanical Gardens (Second oldest in the Western Hemisphere)
- Morant Bay Lighthouse

Trelawny - Trelawny is bordered by the parishes of St Ann in the east, St James in the west, and St Elizabeth and Manchester in the south. Most of the parish is flat, with wide plains such as Queen of Spain's Valley, and Windsor. Trelawny has pockets of rich culture indigenous to the parish. The southern section of Trelawny is a part of the Cockpit Country, and is uninhabitable. It is therefore a natural reserve for flora and fauna; most of Jamaica's 27 endemic bird species can be found there, along with yellow snakes, and the giant swallowtail butterfly, the largest butterfly in the western hemisphere. The main towns are Falmouth, Martha Brae, Stewart's Town, Rio Bueno and Wait-a-Bit.

- An underground spring and watching mystical waters illuminate a tropical night.
- Swamp Safari
- Greenwood Great House
- The Rock Spring Caves and the Quashie River Sink Caves
- Food Tour with Jamaica Culinary Tours
- Stewart Castle in Duncans
- The Baptist Manse on Market Street near the waterfront
- The Reggae to Wear garment factory
- Falmouth Cruise Ship Pier

- Multi-Purpose Complex

Westmoreland - Located at the west end of the island, is adjoined on the north by the parish of Hanover and on the East by St. Elizabeth and St. James. The parish has a combination of white limestone, marl, sand, gravel and coral reefs. Lying on the Georges Plain, the parish is drained by the Cabaritta River. The main towns are Savanna-La-Mar, Negril, Bluefields, Grange Hill, Bethel Town and Seaford Town.

- The Mausoleum at Grange Hill
- The Roaring River and Cave
- Bluefields Beach and Kool Runnings Water Park
- The Great Morass (A large swamp area)
- Seeing the Peter Tosh Memorial

Travel Overview

Now that your kindred spirit have been rekindled and set alight by what you have read and seen so far, natural progression suggests that it is now finally time for you to make that all important vacation plan on this tropical paradise. The great news is that Jamaica offers a vacation for every holidaymaker and every budget no matter your location. Most of the visitors to the island arrive by air and there are connections from major cities in North America, the Caribbean, the United Kingdom and Europe.

In addition, most of world's largest cruise line companies will call at Jamaica's ports throughout the year. Cruise passenger terminals are found in Ocho Rios, Montego Bay, Port Antonio, Falmouth and Kingston. At the time of writing Jamaica continues to receive record cruise calls according to the Jamaican Tourist Board.

There are a number of package holidays available to throughout the year and Jamaican hotels both large and small offer a range of plans with dining and recreation options from All-inclusives to European Plans. Many of these cater to specific niche needs of groups and meetings, families, couples or sport/adventure and have organised tours to many of the attractions across the island. On the other hand if you want to experience activities that speak to your interests there is a plethora of villas, apartments and guesthouses which may provide visitors with greater opportunities to create their own vacation. Most offers may include a combination of self-catering and/or bed and breakfast facilities which provide viable and reasonable alternatives for the shrewd visitor.

Jamaica has modern international airports in both of its cities – Norman Manley International in Kingston and the Sangster International in Montego Bay. When you are flying on an individual basis it is important to ensure which airport is closer to your preferred destination as not all airlines go to both. . Modern port and shipping facilities complement the industry's services to cruise lines and private yachts.

Over the years Jamaica's road network continues to improve and is now one of the most extensive for an island of its size. Highway 2000 links towns in the southern section of the island while the North South Highway incorporate towns on the northern section of the island. There is also a vast array of transportation means available for your individual needs. These range from luxury coaches and limousines to taxis and rental cars. There are also transport companies offering customised tours.

Of course every great trip will need great food and in Jamaica you will be spoilt for choice. Whether it is the mouth-watering dishes, succulent fruits, unique cocktails or refreshing beverages there is always something to suit every taste on offer. If that in itself is not enticing enough, the island has many fine restaurants which offer an array of dining styles in Jamaican, American, Continental, East Indian, Chinese and Italian cuisines, among others.

Part III: Symbols, People, Places and Things

So let us take a quick glance at the prime experience on offer at the major resort areas beginning with the capital Kingston. It is important to note that a modern transportation system provides ease of travel between and in resort areas.

Kingston - provides opportunities for natural, historical, cultural experiences as well as well as numerous entertainment and recreational facilities.

Montego Bay - the tourist capital of Jamaica as all the very best that Jamaica has to offer including five championship golf courses, boutique and luxury hotels, themed restaurants and gaming lounges as well as picture-perfect white sand beaches.

Ocho Rios - located on the North Coast in the parish of St. Ann is home many world renowned attractions. It provides a lush landscape of caves, gardens, rivers white sand beaches and offers a variety of cultural experiences.

Negril - a beach resort town located across two parishes - Westmoreland and Hanover - is one of the most popular tourist destinations in Jamaica and home to some of the most adorable hotels and stunning white sand beaches in the island. There are also pubs with live reggae music and local fare that cater to all budgets and tastes.

South Coast – Known for its natural mineral healing baths, rocky cliffs, beautiful unique dark sandy beaches, rich history and authentic culture. From Manchester across the more temperate flatlands of St. Elizabeth, the South Coast is plantations and safaris, small intimate communities, rustic, comfortable inns, fresh produce and provisions. It also host to Appleton Estate and the unique flavour of Jamaica birthed in the cool, lush Nassau Valley and the people who make it the world's finest rum.

Port Antonio – Portland's capital was originally settled by the Spaniards. This town is popular for its unblemished beauty, lush landscape and bio-diversity. It is the hideaway for some of Jamaica's most exclusive tourist accommodations. Port Antonio is also a yachter's haven with a modern marina, named in honour of Errol Flynn, and dry dock facility. Jamaica's longest running fishing tournament – the Port Antonio Marlin Tournament – takes place in the area each October.

Runaway Bay - Runaway bay is situated in the middle of Jamaica's north coast. It lies east of Ocho Rios and Montego Bay is to the west. The crystal clear water and sugar- white sand beaches are a joy to behold.

The resort area also encompasses the town of Falmouth with its fine examples of Georgian architecture and the Jamaican vernacular. The sleepy seaside town of Falmouth dates back to the early 1700s and was served by piped potable water before many major North American cities, including New York.

GLOSSARY

Afi – has/have to
Agaen – again
Ah – at/it is
Ah fi – it belongs to
Ah good – Serves you right
Ahoa - Oh
Aise – ears
Alms ouse – nonsense
Anansi – spider
Anodda – another
Ar – her
Av – have
Ax – ask
Baaskit – basket
Backa – behind
Backle – bottle
Bad mout –speak ill of
Bad mine – jealous/grudgeful
Bakansa – sharp answer, retort
Bafan – clumsy/awkward
Bandoolo – dishonest/dishonesty
Bangarang – disturbance/noise
Bankra – big basket
Barn – born
Bat – moth
Battam – bottom
Beanie – small
Befoe – before
Ben de – was/were
Berry – very
Bex – upset/angry
Bickle – food

Bickle – food
Big and so-so-so – big-bodied and lazy
Bline – blind
Brawta – extra
Breda – brother
Breshé – breadfruit
Bruk – break/broke
Bud – bird
Bun – burn
Bun – burn
Buss - burst
Bwile – boil
Bwoy – boy
Cackroach – cockroach
Carry-go bring-come – gossip
Cawna – corner
Chowziz – pants
Chuck – truck
Chupid – stupid
Cliding – cloying
Cobich – mean/stingy
Coco – cocoa
Com yah – come here
Coodeh – look at that
Craben – craven
Crakup - laugh
Cratch – scratch
Crawny – look awful
Crawses – problematic situation/ someone who causes problems
Cruff – untidy/non-ambitious
Cry-cry – easily upset/cries a lot

Cumbulo – peers
Cumfat - comfort
Cunnyman – conman
Cunue – canoe
Cuss – to quarrel
Cuss-cuss – quarrel
Cut yeye – to look at someone in disdain
Cuya – look at this
Cyaan – cannot
Dan – than
Danki – donkey
Dat – that
Dawg – dog
De - the
Deble – devil
ded lef – inheritance
Dégé dégé – only
Deh – there/is
Deh deh – is there
De bout – around, nearby
Dem – them
Di – the
Diay – day
Doah – door
Doan – don't
Dongkia – carefree
Doze – those
Dress back – step back/reverse
Dung – down
Duont it? – isn't that so?
Duppy – ghost
Dut – earth/soil
Dutty – dirty
Dweet – do it
Ebery – every
Ih – it
Ih-he – yes
Ef - if
Ef a so, a so – so be it
Facety – feisty/saucy
Fah – for
Fall dung – fall
Fallaw – follow
Fala bak a mi – follow me
Fambily – family
Farrid – forehead
Fass – inquisitive
Fasser - faster
Fedda – feather
Fenké fenké – slight/weak
Fi – for/to
Fiah – fire
Firetick – fire-stick
Fiwi – ours
Flim – film
Fluxy – flaccid/squashy
Fool-fool – silly/stupid
Foot bottam – sole of the foot
Force ripe – unnaturally mature
Frak tail – hemline
Frouzi – smelly
Fur – far
Gaah farin - go abroad
Gahlang – go on
Gastu – must
Get chruu – succeed
Ghana – going to (place)
Ginal – trickster/dishonest
Gi a six fi a nain – deceive
Goh – go
Goh dung – go down
Gonna – going to…
Gravalicious – greedy
Grung – ground/cultivated field
Guweh – go away
Gwaan – go on
Gwine – going to
Gyal – girl
Haad – hard
Hab – has/have
Hackle – hassle/bother

Glossary

Haffi – have/has to
Halla – holler/cry out loudly
Han – hand
Han middle – palm
Hat - painful
Hea - hear
Head top – crown of the head
Hebby – heavy
Heng – hang
Henka – hanging around for food
Hitey titey – snobbish
Hush – be comforted
Ih – It
Ih-ih – no
Im – him
Inna – In /Into
Jankro – vulture/crow
Jankro Batty – Unpurified white rum
Jing-bang – lots of useless items
Jook – pierce/poke
Jrap fut – to dance
Juck - pierce
Junjo – mould
Kak op – to raise
Keba – cover
Kekkle – kettle/boiling pot
Ketch – catch/caught
Kibba - cover
Kin pupalick – to do a somersault
Kin teet – grin
Kot ten – to sit with legs crossed
Krai krii – to call time-out
Krismus – Christmas
Kuh ya – look here
Kumoochin – stingy/mean
Kuul-yu-fut – relax
Kya – care
labba labba – gossip

Laffi-laffi – giggly
Laka se - as if
Lang – long
Langa – longer
Larn – learn
Lenky – lanky
Lib – live
Libati tekin – presumptious attitude
Libba – liver
Lick - hit
Licky licky – suck up/greedy
Likkle – little
Lilly – little
Limba - limber
Lob – love
Lyad – liar
Ma – mother/madam
Macca – thorn
Mada – mother
Maggige – maggot
Mannas – manners
Mash up – destroy/break up
Maskitta – mosquito
Massa – mister
Mawga – meagre /malnourished
Meja - measure
Mek – make
Memba – remember
Mi – me
Miehke-miehke – messy/distasteful
Mikhase – hurry up
Mout – mouth
Mout-a-massy – someone who talks too much
Mucky – filthy
Mumma – mother
Munstah – monster
Mussi – must
Muss-muss – mouse
Naah – not going to

Jamaican Proverbs and Places and Symbols

Nebber – never
Nize – noise
Noh – does not
Nowey - nowhere
Nuff – plenty/brazen
Nutten – nothing
Nutting – nothing
Nyam – eat
Oddah – other
Ooman – woman
Outa haada – rude, impudent
Out fi – about to
Owna – owner
Packi - vessel made from a gourd
Pan – on
Passa passa – mix up
Patoo – owl
PawPaw – papaya
Peenywally – firefly
Peteta – potato
Pickney – young child
Picky-picky – choosey/sparse
Poah – poor
Poppyshow – laughable/show off
Pread – spread
Prekeh – someone who thinks a lot of himself but is in fact a laughing stock
Pupa – father
Pushi – push it
Puss – cat
Putto-putto – soft
Puttus – sweetheart
Pwoil – spoil
Pyaa-pyaa – sickly/feeble
Quint – blink
Ramp – play
Red yeye – envious
Renk – foul smell/rude
Rivva – river
Roun – around

Run boat – informal cooking
Sa – sir
Sabe – save
Saggle – saddle
Sake a – because of
Seame weigh – just like that
Sarry – sorry
Seh feh – dare me
Shaat – short
Shaata – shorter
Shedda – shadow
Sheg up – to disappoint, unreliable
Shi – she
Shuub – shove/push
Si – see
Siddong – sit down
Sinting – something
Slackniss – lewd/vulgar behaviour
Sleep up – coagulate
Smaddy – somebody
Soppm – something
Sopsy – weak/soft/puny
Spirit tek – have affinity
Stranja – stranger
Stush – snobbish
Se-se – gossip
Su-su – to gossip
Swallaw – swallow
Stush – snobbish
Su-su – carry news/gossip
Swo-so – mediocre
Tallawah – Impressive
Tan – stand/stay/is
Tan deh – stay there
Tan up – stand up
Tap – Stop/top
Tea – any hot drink
Teddy – steady
Tegereg – person of no class/uncouth
Tek – take

Glossary

Tenk yuh – thank you
Tick – stick
Ticker – thicker
Ticky ticky – young children /fish
Tideh – today
Ting – thing
Togeda – together
Trampooz – to walk about
Trow – throw
Trubble – trouble
Tun – turn
Uhnu – you all
Umhm – yes
Waagen? – what else?
Waah - want
Wah – what
Wallah – wallow
Warra warra – (used instead of a curseword)
Wash – sugar mixed with water
Wats – what's
Weh – where/away
Wha – what
Wha-ah gwaan – what's going on
Wha mek – how come/why
Whappen – what's up?
Wi – we
Wid – with
Wingy – small/feeble
Wod – word
Woss – worse/worst
Wosser – worse
Wuk – work
Wukliss – worthless
Yah - here
Yasso – here
Yeye – eye
Yout – youth
Yuh – you

INDEX

Alligator, 192
Anancy, 7, 71, 142
Ants, 9
Beetle, 9
Blood, 11, 140, 155, 176, 186
Bowl, 11
Bucket, 11
Bud, 11, 102, 199
Bull, 192
Cane, 194
Cat, 12
Chicken, 12, 184
Chink, 12
Chip, 12
Christmas, 7, 180, 201
Clock, 188
Cockroach, 12
Corn, 180, 186
Cow, 13, 179
Coward, 176, 193
Crab, 13, 14
Crow, 44, 107, 193
Dance, 104, 134, 136, 140, 142
Deaf ears, 16
Dirt, 21
Disease, 158
Dog, 10, 15, 186
Donkey, 22, 184
Drunk, 22
Duck, 23
Duppy, 23, 186, 200
Eat, 23, 82
Eye, 29, 146
Eye lash, 29

Family, 9, 11, 147, 150, 151
Finger, 29, 107, 194
Fire, 29, 30, 141
Fish, 30, 133
Fool, 30, 200
Foot, 200
Fowl, 30, 31
Fox, 31, 176
Goat, 178
God, 10, 24, 31, 81, 83, 123, 124
Grass, 186
Hair, 156
Hand, 122
Hawk, 102, 184
Head, 153, 186, 187, 201
Heart, 123, 143, 153
Hog, 33, 186
Hole, 190
Honey, 141
Horse, 94
Hungry, 33
Jackass, 80, 82
Lawyer, 150, 152
Leaf, 186
Lion, 141
Lizard, 46
Mango, 108, 182
Market, 105, 146, 188, 191, 192, 194
Milk, 141, 187
Money, 53, 146
Mongoose, 185
Monkey, 39, 53
Moon, 108, 166

Parson, 59
Peacock, 59
Pen, 164, 187, 189, 190
Pickney, 60, 202
Pudding, 180
Puss, 61, 95, 202
Rain, 62
Rat, 62, 190
River, 50, 51, 52, 64, 165, 187, 190, 191, 192, 193, 194, 195
Rope, 141
Rum, ix, 180
Skin, 134
Sleep, 103, 202
Soup, 180
Steer, 57
Tiger, 148
Time, 16, 70, 104, 106, 108, 130, 141, 172
Tree, 70, 71, 90, 110, 117, 183, 188
Trouble, 71
Turkey, 145
Water, 96, 113, 157, 180, 190, 193, 195
Weed, 186
Well, 140
Wing, 140

REFERENCES

www.jamaica-gleaner.com/gleaner/20061212/lead/lead1.html
www.discoverjamaica.com/history7.htm
www.jis.gov.jm/gov_ja/history.asp
https://jis.gov.jm/
https://www.jtbonline.org/
www.jamaicans.com/jamaicansoverseas/
www.districtleaderspodcast.org/wordpress/2009/03/02/ep-33-dr-beverly-
www.jamaica-gleaner.com/pages/history/
www.atlantapublicschools.us/18611010892250280/site/default.asp
www.my-island-jamaica.com/index.html
www.jamaica-gleaner.com/gleaner/20081012/out/out6.html
www.calabashfestival.org/pages/artists/artists_page/anthony_winkler.html
www.news.ncu.edu.jm/news_item.aspx?NewsID=1040
www.billmorris.info/
www.100greatblackbritons.com/list.html
www.jamaicans.com/info/heroes.htm
www.jis.gov.jm/special_sections/Heroes/Heroes.htm
www.jamaica2rhatid.com/index.php?title=Jamaica
www.jamaicapage.com/jamaica-national-symbols/
www.caribbean-junky.com/jamaica/mandeville.htm
www.thirdworldband.com/
rastaseed.com/2009/02/16/rasta-jamaican-medicine-fever-grass-aka-lemon-
www.jamaica-gleaner.com/gleaner/20030217/flair/flair2.html

www.jamaicans.com/culture/articles_culture/

www.jamaicans.com/articles/primearticles/saving-the-jamaican-iguan.shtml

www.jamaicamax.com/tag/jamaica-crocodile/

www.jis.gov.jm/special_sections/Independence/anthem&Pledge.html

www.jamaica-gleaner.com/gleaner/20061212/lead/lead1.html

www.discoverjamaica.com/history7.htm

www.jis.gov.jm/gov_ja/history.asp

www.jamaicans.com/jamaicansoverseas/

www.atlantapublicschools.us/18611010892250280/site/default.asp

www.jamaica-gleaner.com/gleaner/20081012/out/out6.html

www.jamaicans.com/jamaicansoverseas/atlant/atlantajamaicanDrBWaineKo

http://en.wikipedia.org/wiki/Jamaican_Canadian

http://en.wikipedia.org/wiki/Jamaican_American

http://randb.about.com/od/gthroughm/p/Mya.htm

www.inoutstar.com/news/Alicia-J-Augello-Cook-aka-Alicia-Keys-2354.html

www.alicia-zone.net/

www.jamaica-gleaner.com/gleaner/20060322/business/business1.html

en.wikipedia.org/wiki/List_of_Jamaicans

www.jamaica-gleaner.com/gleaner/20060423/out/out2.html

www.occba.net/barnett.html

www.caribbeancourtofjustice.org/commission/barnett.html#

www.jamaicans.com/articles/primeinterviews/RainaSimoneInterview.shtml

www.nlj.gov.jm/?q=docs/outstandingja_bib.htm

www.jis.gov.jm/default.asp

www.allmusic.com/cg/amg.dll?p=amg&sql=11:grk9ikk6bbc9~T1

References

www.timesonline.co.uk/tol/comment/obituaries/article541898.ece

www.caricom.org/jsp/projects/personalities/sir_philip_sherlock.jsp?menu=project

www.yardflex.com/archives/004675.html

www.jis.gov.jm/special_sections/This%20Is%20Jamaica/rondolph.html

www.jtbonline.org/resources/Media%20Kits/Info%20-%20The%20Arts.pdf

www.wjh.harvard.edu/soc/faculty/patterson/

myspot.mona.uwi.edu/proffice/newsroom/entry/3703

www.jm.undp.org/node/146

www.udel.edu/vp-sec/bio_members.html

www.freddiemcgregor.com/biography.html

http://en.wikipedia.org/wiki/Dennis_Brown

www.tootsandthemaytals.com/shopcontent.asp?type=biography

www.musicianguide.com/biographies/1608002621/Dennis-Brown.html#ixzz0i5xvpLII

www.allmusic.com/cg/amg.dll?p=amg&sql=11:3zfuxqy5ldke~T1

http://en.wikipedia.org/wiki/Rex_Nettleford

www.jamaica-gleaner.com/gleaner/20100314/ent/ent4.html

www.jamaica-gleaner.com/gleaner/20070211/ent/ent5.html

www.biographybase.com/biography

www.newnationrising.com//Wailer_Bunny.html

www.reggae-reggae.co.uk/go/levi-roots

www.goldgenie.com/laban-bio.php

en.wikipedia.org/wiki/Shabba_Ranks

www.windiescricket.com/index.cfm?objectID=AE134605-A791-FAB3-517C5CA74A2634C9&pageid=F89A3DCB-CD30-AE66-262FEDAACC197145&category=EA23B92F-C0A8-03C6-5A83DD2DB9698173

news.bbc.co.uk/1/hi/entertainment/7820786.stm

http://www.nlj.gov.jm/bios-n-z#seacole

www.jamaicans.com/articles/primeinterviews/interview-with-jamaican-photographer-ray-chen.shtml

www.bbc.co.uk/whodoyouthinkyouare/new-stories/ainsley-harriott/how-we-did-it_1.shtml

www.dailymail.co.uk/tvshowbiz/article-1054853/Theo-Walcott-national-hero--ask-mum-let-in.html

www.somaliaonline.com/cgi-bin/ubb/ultimatebb.cgi?ubb=get_topic;f=1;t=000531;p=0

www.speakerscorner.co.uk/file/808904a07335860300d9cf79520e0e56/ainsley-harriot-chef-cook-tv-recipes-books-celebrity.html

biography.jrank.org/pages/2351/Holmes-Kelly.html

www.famouspeople.co.uk/k/kellyholmes.html

www.lonympics.co.uk/ts.htm

www.jamaicaobserver.com/entertainment/Fashion-mogul-to-be-honoured_7473896

www.blacklifemagazine.com/

www.dartmouth.edu/~lhc/events/2009/cooper.html

www.jamaica-gleaner.com/gleaner/20090928/flair/flair3.html

www.jamaica-gleaner.com/gleaner/200702

http://www.jamaica-gleaner.com/gleaner/20090726/ent/ent1.html07/cleisure/cleisure1.html

www.jamaica-gleaner.com/gleaner/20081017/news/news6.html

http://www.ba

www.caymannetnews.com/Archive/Archive%20Articles/January%202002/Issue%20139/2002%20New%20Years%20honour.html

lancingjusticewithfairness.com/experienceandawards.html

www.dare-to-dream-1994.com/

www.icelebz.com/celebs/jamelia/biography.html

en.wikipedia.org/wiki/Jamelia

www.jis.gov.jm/special_sections/This%20Is%20Jamaica/bolt.html

References

www.jncb.com/corp_info/bod.asp

www.caribbeannetnews.com/cgi-script/csArticles/articles/000059/005916.htm

www.acneinblackwomen.com/interview.html

drpersadsingh.com/

www.vendryeswellnesscenter.com/credentials.html

www.vendryeswellnesscenter.com/credentials.html

www.jamaica-gleaner.com/gleaner/20061210/ent/ent2.html

www.artistdirect.com/artist/bio/mutabaruka/471721

www2.carleton.ca/neuroscience/news/patrice-smith-published-in-the-journal-

www2.carleton.ca/newsroom/news-releases/carleton-professor-finds-real-world-solution-to-nerve-damage/

www.jamaica-gleaner.com/gleaner/20090302/news/news3.html

www.jis.gov.jm/foreign_affairs/html/20091103T110000-0500_21743_JIS_JAMAICAN_BORN_POLICEMAN_APPOINTED__DEPUTY_CHIEF_OF_TORONTO_POLICE.asp

www.jamaica-gleaner.com/gleaner/20090302/news/news2.html

www.jamaica-gleaner.com/gleaner/20030725/ent/ent1.html

www.jamaica-gleaner.com/gleaner/20080504/ent/ent1.html

www.jamaica-gleaner.com/gleaner/20051030/ent/ent3.html

www.mobile.jamaicagleaner.com/20090330/ent/ent1.php

www.jamaica-gleaner.com/gleaner/20070615/ent/ent6.html

www.nasa.gov/centers/marshall/news/news/releases/2007/07-100.html

www.jamaica-gleaner.com/gleaner/20100411/sports/sports9.html

www.jamaica-gleaner.com/gleaner/20080512/flair/flair3.html

www.gleaner.com/gleaner/20070308/phenomenal/phenomenal24.html

http://jamaica-gleaner.com/article/news/20151120/bio-tech-lays-foundation-international-medical-breakthrough

http://www.jamaicaobserver.com/news/jamaican-born-lawyer-jeffrey-fraser-gets-us-honour_116700?profile=1373&template=MobileArticle

http://www.jamaicaobserver.com/news/Daughter-of-eminent-Jamaican-lawyer-Ian-Ramsay-sworn-in-as-chief-justice-of-Turks---Caicos

http://www.jamaicaobserver.com/columns/Barrington-Watson--A-life-in-paint

http://old.jamaica-gleaner.com/gleaner/20020428/arts/arts1.html

https://literature.britishcouncil.org/writer/james-berry

http://jamaica-gleaner.com/gleaner/20130318/ent/ent1.html

https://www.independent.co.uk/news/people/obituary-professor-m-g-smith-

https://www.theguardian.com/stage/2012/jan/16/barry-reckord

https://aalbc.com/authors/author.php?author_name=Kellie+Magnus

https://www.youtube.com/watch?v=blJY8-aF0mQ

https://www.biography.com/people/susan-rice-391616

https://www.imdb.com/name/nm0004734/

http://www.jamaicaobserver.com/style/canadian-senate-welcomes-jamaican-dr-rosemary-moodie_154919?profile=1606

https://animals.mom.me/snakes-jamaica-6540.html

https://www.planetware.com/jamaica/top-rated-beaches-in-jamaica-jam--.htm

www.ingramcontent.com/pod-product-compliance
Lightning Source LLC
Chambersburg PA
CBHW040426250426
43661CB00025BA/1315/J